Creating Documentation in an Agile Scrum Environment

I0016256

Marni Helene Nispel

Copyright

Disclaimer

The information contained in this book is provided on an "as is" basis, without warranty. Although the author and publisher have made every effort to ensure that the information in this book was correct at press time, the author and publisher do not assume, and hereby disclaim, any liability to any party for any loss, damage, or disruption caused by errors or omissions, whether such errors or omissions result from negligence, accident, or any other cause.

This book contains links to third-party websites that are not under the control of the author and are provided to you for convenience only. The inclusion of a link in this book does not imply that the author endorses, or accepts responsibility for, the content of the third-party sites, or to services, information, or products that they provide.

Trademarks

JIRA® is a Registered Trademark of Atlassian®.
All trademarks are the property of their respective owners.

This book is dedicated to my dad,
William Nispel,
who believed in me every moment of my life.

While he never saw this book published, my father knew it was in its final stages. When I knew he wasn't coming home, I told him about this dedication. I wanted him to know what a difference he made in my world; he smiled.

The following is the end of the eulogy that I gave for him. I think it makes a fitting start to this book.

> "If you take nothing else from my Dad's life, please take this: Respect yourself. Respect others. Get to know people. Take pride in others. And always leave a room, a home, a job, a person, or the world better than they were before. I know he did."

About the author

© Photo by Kimberly Brinkley/JSM Photography

Marni Nispel is a veteran of the documentation field and continues to work, learning and honing a craft she loves.

This book is her first, and possibly her last (based on the time it took to create). She has a master's degree in Technical and Professional Writing from Northeastern University and has nearly completed a master's degree in Industrial and Organizational Psychology at Walden University.

Marni's proudest accomplishment (even more than this book) is her daughter, Kyri, who has a bachelor's degree in Counseling Psychology, focusing on children with anxiety-based challenges. Kyri has her own business helping people with anxiety: https://TwelfthHouseCoaching.com

Marni lives in Massachusetts with her husband, Tim, who is working on his own (far more interesting) book, and their dog, Athena.

Contact the author with your feedback: PrimalNines@gmail.com

Acknowledgements

I want to thank my husband, Tim Curran, for believing in me and encouraging me.

I have to thank Cindy Morell for editing a book on a topic about which she knew absolutely nothing, and was not excited about in any way. That's love.

Of course, I need to acknowledge my mother, Mary Jo Nispel, for reading and editing this book not once, but twice. I also need to thank her for encouraging me during some of the toughest times. As I mentioned in the dedication, my father passed away months before I finished this book. She is the picture of strength. She loved and supported me every moment. I'm eternally grateful for her occasionally asking me, "How's the book coming?" when she knew full well I had just about given up.

Paul Duncan, Steve Ruo, Benjamin Muise, and Denise Dickenson for talking Scrum with me constantly while I developed this book, for helping me more clearly understand Scrum and Agile, and for helping me fine-tune the details in making Documentation work in that environment. While we didn't always agree, the conversations were always enlightening. Any errors in the explanation of Agile and Scrum are purely mine. All the information on the application of Scrum to Documentation is mine based on my experience. The fact that I talked with them in no way means that they endorse any of the advice I give or any of the statements I make.

Contents

Documentation in Scrum   87

Where does Documentation fit?...............88

Extras   209

Introduction

About this book

Why did I write this book?

I've been asked over and over how to make Documentation work with Agile (particularly Scrum), and the key word really is *with*.

The role of writers in Agile is frequently under debate, so it's best to begin with an open mind. As many Agile and Scrum experts have explained, Agile and Scrum can be used for anything from developing software to remodeling a home. So, clearly, Documentation can be developed using this framework. The question is: how?

When done right, Agile (Scrum) can be extremely beneficial to Documentation. With the right processes in place, you can alleviate some of the typical problems you face. For example, you know how it's almost impossible to get reviews done in a timely fashion? With the right process, that is no longer an issue thanks to Scrum.

Context

I wrote this book on the assumption that you are part of the Product Development or Engineering Team and that you are integrating in some way into Scrum teams. If that is not the case, this book can still be extremely helpful. First, it will help you understand how the Scrum teams in Product Development work. Second, it can help you prepare for a future job where you are integrated into those Scrum teams. Finally, as I explain later in the book, Scrum is an excellent tool for an Information Engineering Team to manage a workload. In this last case, you can simply concentrate on the areas focused on an Information Engineering Team's use of Scrum.

What this book is

This book is...

- A collection of ideas and experiences.
- The culmination of learning through trial and error at a variety of companies. I'm going to tell you what has worked for me, my colleagues, and my teams over the years.
- What I've found to be best practices, and the history and reasoning behind them. I've put in a lot of trial and error. So, let me save you the effort and agony.
- A survival guide for writers in an Agile Scrum environment.

What this book is NOT

This book is not...

- A step-by-step "How To" guide.
- Intended to provide all the answers or provide a foolproof process for successfully navigating Agile Scrum.

- An intensive discussion of Agile Scrum. For that, you should consult any of the many books written on that topic.

This book may not be for you if...

This book and its ideas may not work for you if:

- You have very small Scrum teams.
- Your product has very few customer features.
- Your company does not use Agile and never plans to.

If any or all of these apply, then this book may provide too much process to be useful. But then you probably wouldn't have purchased this book. You're reading this book because you need, or believe you will need, to navigate Agile.

How to use this book

As with almost everything I've ever written in my daily job, and probably almost everything you've ever written, this book is not intended to be read straight through in a linear fashion.

If you know all about Agile, you can probably skip the *Agile Scrum 101* section and move on to section titled "*Where does Documentation fit?*" (page 88), which presents several ways of doing Documentation with Scrum.

Conventions

Throughout this book, I break with standard conventions and styles, but there is a method to my madness.

- The word "documentation" has different meanings. For simplicity and clarity, I use the following terminology.

  o Documentation as the all-encompassing concept of our field. "I've been in the documentation field for more years than I care to admit." For the purposes of this book, I capitalize it: *Documentation*.

  o The team. We are often referred to as the Documentation Team, or just Documentation. "Hey, can someone run this by Documentation to see what they need?" For the purposes of this book, I refer to this as the *Information Engineering Team*. It helps eliminate confusion and is the title of the team where I once worked.

  o A specific item of documentation. We create an online help system, a single help topic, an entire guide, or just a single paragraph. For the purposes of this book, I refer to those as a *documentation product.*

- o Except for references to the Agile Manifesto, "documentation" always means your customer documentation product. If I mean the artifacts that developers create (such as specifications and plans), I specify that.

  - ▪ "Customers" are anyone who uses your documentation product, whether they are internal or external to your company.

- I capitalize words that are important terms and concepts, even if conventional wisdom and style may indicate that they shouldn't be capitalized.

- When necessary, I use the future tense, such as the word "will" because I am actually talking about things that will happen... in the future. (If you're doing the work *while* reading this, as if it were a recipe, we need to talk.)

- Occasionally, I use capitalization and bold (and even underline) because I think something is important and I want to emphasize it.

- I sometimes split my infinitives, leave dangling participles, use contractions, and I may even resort to using passive voice if I deem it necessary for clarity and simplicity.

- I call us writers. I'm aware of the variety of titles we hold. I even created the Title Generator below, which I once posted on LinkedIn®. For simplicity, I use writer.

"Technical Writer" Title Generator

Column 1	Column 2
Pick one or more	Pick one
Communications	Architect
Content	Author
Documentation	Coordinator
Information	Designer
Publications	Developer
Technical[1]	Engineer
User[1]	Expert
User Assistance	Specialist
Writing[2]	Strategist
	Writer
Less likely but not out of the question	
Language	Artiste
Text	Boss
Word	Craftsperson
	Guru
	Diva/Divo
	Ninja
	Slinger
	Wizard

[1]With the exception of Technical Writer, this must be followed by another option from Column 1.

[2]This cannot be followed by Writer.

- I use "they" as a gender-neutral pronoun. There are too many people in the world for whom gender-based pronouns are a real issue. This is especially true in my little corner of the world. This is 2019 and we can let go of our school grammar lessons. "They" can be a single individual. A friend once told me to think about the car in front of you when you're driving somewhere. "What are they doing?! They're an idiot!" "Did you see how they avoided that cow? They're awesome!" Once you start using it, you'll be amazed how easy it is. And you never know who'll appreciate it.

Basically, if there is something here that makes the editor in you start to twitch, just know that my editor twitched too, and I overruled them.

Your tools

Many experts have discussed how well Agile and DITA work together. If you'd like more information on those topics, the *Bibliography* on page 235 contains lots of suggestions.

To use this book, you don't have to be working with DITA. The strategies I developed were created in a variety of very different environments. Similarly, these strategies will work regardless of your writing method, authoring tools, and your output mediums. Authoring tools are just that, they're the tools you use to create your product, just as developers write code in a certain language and QA has test frameworks that they use.

This is about the process surrounding your writing.

- How do you get what you need?
- How do you provide your product to the team?

- How do you gather and incorporate feedback?
- How do you get to "done"?

Planning and Tracking Software

Within this book, you'll notice that I use JIRA (from Atlassian) for examples and processes. I use JIRA because that is the software that I've used most recently and most often; so, it's what I know.

Your company may use other software for planning and tracking. That software may have similar functionality or the ability to customize to create these processes. I would suggest, more than anything, that you learn how to use your company's planning and tracking software. Learn how to:

- report bugs (defects)
- create epics, stories, tasks, and sub-tasks
- view dashboards, sprints, and Agile boards

You're going to be in that software every day, so you should know what developers, QA, and Product Managers know and you should be able to use the same language they do.

TIP: Learn how to run queries. This will save you time. I have my own dashboard with saved queries in various shapes and forms for all sorts of "automated" tracking. This will make you more organized and more efficient.

Agile Scrum

Agile Scrum 101

This section is intended to provide an overview of Agile (and Scrum in particular) as well as the language and flow of it. This is for Agile in general and does not provide Documentation-specific information. The role of the Information Engineering Team is explained in subsequent sections.

This is only an overview of Agile and Scrum. If you want more information, there is a vast library available. You can start with the items in the *Bibliography* on page 235.

Why do I need to know about Agile?

This is the most important part of the book, and not because this book is titled *Creating Documentation in an Agile Scrum Environment.* It's important because you need a complete understanding of what Agile is, so you can understand your place in it. You must know the rules of engagement before you step into battle.

So, what is Agile? What does it mean? What doesn't it mean?

At this point, it doesn't matter if you're currently working in an Agile environment. In fact, if you're not, this might be even more helpful because you'll be able to get an understanding that isn't filtered through a company's interpretation. That also means that you may be able to head off some problems before they start or, at least, you can get a better process in place.

However, if you are already in an Agile environment, you still need a good understanding of what Agile is, so you can help develop (or direct) a process for Documentation that still meets Agile criteria.

So, here's the question: Do you know what Agile is?

If you're positive that you do, then you can skip the rest of this section and go directly to *"Where does Documentation fit?"* on page 88. If you're not sure, you have no clue, you think it just means "flexible", or you want a refresher, read on.

What is Agile?

Starting with the basics, Agile is an iterative approach to developing software quickly and efficiently. It started with the Agile Manifesto. Here is what the manifesto actually says:

Manifesto for Agile Software Development

We are uncovering better ways of developing software by doing it and helping others do it.

Through this work we have come to value:

Individuals and interactions over processes and tools

Working software over comprehensive Documentation

Customer collaboration over contract negotiation

Responding to change over following a plan

That is, while there is value in the items on the right,
we value the items on the left more.

(http://www.agilemanifesto.org)

For such a small piece, there is a lot of information and some very large concepts. Notice what is not there. There is no prescriptive process. There is no set of rules or prescribed working structure. The manifesto never says what you must do, nor even what you should do, and it certainly does not say what you can't do. It is simply a list of values or preferences.

Agile was developed as an alternative to Waterfall, where the work was handed off almost in a conveyor-belt fashion. Planning and designing were done first. Next the development was done. After the product was completely developed, it was handed over to QA. Usually, the Information Engineering Team would create their documentation product at the very end. (Allow me an aside here to say that Waterfall has been vilified over the years. It is not evil. It is not guaranteed to fail, in the right place. And it does have its place. However, that place is not in most software development companies.)

As Agile was implemented, several variants emerged from the Agile umbrella:

- Scrum
- Kanban
- XP
- and many others

This book focuses on Scrum because it is the most common; therefore, it's the one you're most likely to encounter in your career. Also, that is the one I'm most familiar with and it's the environment in which I developed these strategies.

Remember, Agile and therefore Scrum, is not a methodology. It is simply a framework or an approach; it's a process for continuous improvement. "Scrum is the framework I built to put those [manifesto] values into practice. There is no methodology" (Sutherland, *Scrum: The Art*, p13).

True Agile

It's important to know one key piece of information before you start trying to find your place in an Agile environment: **No company is completely Agile!** (Yep, I said it!)

Think of Agile as being similar to enlightenment in Buddhism. There are a set of principles and values. People try to reach enlightenment by continuously improving, but no one ever reaches pure enlightenment; likely, it is an unachievable goal. But the process of trying to reach that goal makes you better. In Buddhism, it makes you a better person. In Agile, it makes you a better team.

Every company is at a different level of Agile maturity. Every company has multiple teams doing Agile in multiple ways. That's okay. Companies and teams incorporate areas of Agile that are applicable or helpful, continually adding new steps as they progress.

So, a little foreshadowing, when you start your Documentation process in Agile, you may hear "that's not Scrum" or "that's not Agile." Ask them, in the nicest way possible, why they believe that. They may be correct, and you may have to adjust your methods, or you might have to ask for a little leeway due to extenuating circumstances. They may be wrong, and you'll have to help them understand the error of their ways. (Just between us, I can assure you that there are other ways in which they are not "true Agile.")

Scrum Process Flow

On the surface, Scrum is a simple process. However, it can be complicated in the details and, initially, it can be difficult to understand. That's why there are so many classes, websites, webinars, and so forth. Even graphically, it is not easy to represent. If you do a search for images of Scrum (with any of the following: process, model, timeline, flow, diagram), you're likely to find hundreds of options.

Many of them are quite good. However, there always seems to be at least one thing missing from those images. So, after much searching, I discovered the following image, which identifies some key areas that most other images lack. (And it's also slick!)

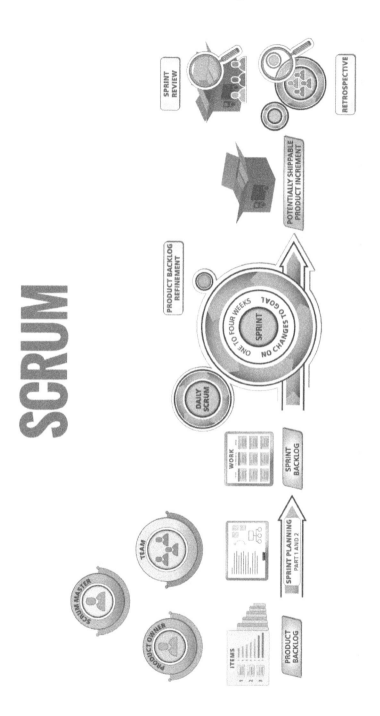

(Courtesy of http://less.works)

Scrum Elements

As I've said, Scrum is an iterative process. It's about working through and repeating several stages. Some you repeat frequently (daily); some you may only do once each release. The following may look overwhelming. I'll define each one as it's used in Scrum and then, in a later chapter, I'll elaborate on how Documentation fits that element.

Release Initiation

The first three steps are generally done outside the scope of the Scrum Team, usually at the corporate level. Only the last step in this section is the creation of the Scrum Team.

1. Determine the *Product Vision and Roadmap* (page 45)
2. Define the *Epics* (page 46)
3. Create an initial *Product Backlog* (page 48)
4. Define *Scrum Teams* (page 50)

Scrum Team work

1. Agree on the *Definition of Ready* (page 54)
2. Agree on the *Definition of Done* (page 55)
3. Before sprint work
   Before you begin any sprint work, update the backlog.
   a. Create new *Stories* (and sometimes new *Epics*, see above) as necessary (page 56)
   b. Groom and point stories (page 62)
   c. Determine the *Sprint Backlog* (page 76)
4. During each sprint
   a. Work and hold *Daily Stand-up Meetings* (page 79)
   b. Bugs (Defects (page 85)
   c. Continue updating the *Product Backlog* (page 48)
5. End of each sprint
   a. *Sprint Review* or Sprint Demo (page 81)
   b. Sprint *Retrospective* (page 83)

End of a Release

1. (Optional) *Hardening (Stabilization) Sprint* (page 62)
2. Release your product to customers
3. Return to Release Initiation work

Product Vision and Roadmap

The Product Vision is generally done at a higher level than the Scrum Team. It determines the type of product or the result of the Scrum effort, what needs it will address, what differentiates it from existing options, and what are the key attributes that will make it a success.

The roadmap looks at the major milestones only as a guide. It will likely contain multiple "releases" (results) of the Scrum effort. It's important to note that this is not set in stone but is rather an educated overview reflecting the best current knowledge.

For the Documentation impact and interaction, refer to *Product Vision and Roadmap* on page 146.

Epics

Epics are simply stories that are too large to manage or to accomplish in a single sprint. Because a piece of work must be able to be completed in a single sprint, an epic must be broken out into individual stories.

Often, one or more epics come from a requirement. The requirement is what the customer wants. For example, a car dealer wants a search on their website. That's a requirement and that must be broken down into epics. In this example, a search for used cars might be one epic, while a search for new cars might be a second epic.

Within those epics are small stories of sufficient size and containing enough information to be completed in a single sprint. Again, using this example, stories might include the ability to search by make, model, color, year, mileage, and so on.

In general, there are two types of epics: user and technical.

- User epics are those done for feature work. The stories contained in a user epic result in a "deliverable product" such as those discussed above.

- A technical epic is for work that is not customer facing. This might be work on the product architecture, research, technical debt, knowledge transfer, etc.

For the Documentation impact and interaction, refer to *Epics* on page 148.

Product Backlog

The Product Backlog is the set of items (known as Product Backlog Items or PBIs) that have not yet been scheduled for a particular sprint. These can include user stories, technical stories, and defects. Occasionally the backlog may contain epics if it is not yet clear that the epic needs to be broken down, or if it is serving as a placeholder for work that has not yet been scoped.

This is basically the "To Do" board from which a team pulls work into their Sprint Backlog.

The Product Owner is responsible for keeping the Product Backlog prioritized so the team knows that the most important work is at the top.

The Product Backlog can be updated at any time. The Sprint Backlog can only be updated before a Sprint Commitment.

For the Documentation impact and interaction, refer to *Product Backlog* on page 150.

Scrum Teams

The team is the key functional group in Scrum and is the most essential part of making Scrum work. As such, Scrum teams have been thoroughly examined and explained in detail in other places. What I present here is a superficial overview. If you want more detail about what makes a good Scrum team, you can start with the items in the *Bibliography* on page 235.

Roles

There are only three official roles on a Scrum team:

- *Scrum Master* — The Scrum Master helps facilitate the Scrum process by organizing meetings, managing discussions, and helping keep the team on track. Most importantly, the Scrum Master serves as a buffer between the team and everyone else, and coordinates with other teams. The Scrum Master escalates the team's concerns to management and mitigates outside influences from interfering with the team. The Scrum Master can be a member of the team, filling the role in addition to their regular work, or they could be a dedicated Scrum Master for whom that is their only role. The Scrum Master cannot be the Product Owner or a manager.

- *Product Owner* — The Product Owner is the voice of the customer. They write the epics and stories, help the team groom stories, provide feedback, and maintain the backlog. The Product Owner cannot be the Scrum Master.

- *Team Member* — The "team members" should be cross-functional and have all the necessary competencies to produce a product including: developers, QA, UX designers, writers (we'll talk more about that), and others.

Self-organization

A Scrum Team is supposed to be self-organizing and yet there is little detail about what self-organizing means. If you think of self-organizing as "a group of people who come up with an idea, become a Scrum Team, determine roles, and then start working," you'll be hard-pressed to find companies that do this.

More likely, your team and your project will be determined by management based on the skill set of the members and on customer need, respectively. You may even be assigned your Scrum Master. The "self-organizing" part of Scrum is that the team works the way they want. "One of the key concepts in Scrum is that the team members decide *themselves* how they're going to do the work" (Sutherland, *Scrum: The Art*, p50).

The members of the team must be allowed the freedom to manage themselves.

> "Critical, but perhaps less celebrated, is the freedom to do your job in the way that

you think best—to have autonomy. On all great teams, it's left to the members to decide how to carry out the goals set by those leading the organization" (Sutherland, *Scrum: The Art*, p48).

Co-location

In an ideal Scrum environment, the entire team should be co-located, meaning they should be in the same office and ideally, if possible, they should even be seated together. This allows for the most efficient, even osmotic, communication.

Due to a variety of business reasons, however, this is one of the first Scrum tenets that is discarded. It is more likely that at least some members of your team will live and work all over the country or even all over the globe.

For the Documentation impact and interaction, refer to *Scrum Teams* on page 152.

Definition of Ready (DoR)

The Definition of Ready (DoR) is an undervalued key to making Scrum work. It is quite simply a team's agreement on what must be included in a story before the story can be brought into a sprint and worked on. Of course, it includes the standard requirements of a story such as persona, request, and reason. Most of the time, it also includes additional information such as acceptance criteria, hardware requirements, identification of outside resources and dependencies. (There might be a statement about Documentation. We'll talk about that later.)

This, along with the Definition of Done (DoD), is an essential element in the integration of Documentation into Scrum.

For the Documentation impact and interaction, refer to *Definition of Ready* on page 156.

Definition of Done (DoD)

The Definition of Done (DoD), much like the Definition of Ready (DoR), is an undervalued key to making Scrum work. It is the team's agreement on what is required before a story can be considered Done. Often, there are company-wide standards for the DoD. Those standards might include: code is peer-reviewed, stories have been tested, known defects are fixed or logged, and so on. In addition, the team will have its own criteria. (There might be a statement about Documentation. We'll talk about that later.)

This, along with the Definition of Ready, is an essential element in the integration of Documentation into Scrum.

For the Documentation impact and interaction, refer to *Definition of Done* on page 159.

Stories

Stories (also known as Product Backlog Items, or PBIs are one of the most important items in Scrum. They are the basic unit of work for a team. In general, there are two kinds of stories: user and technical.

The amount and type of work required for a story will vary and depend on the type of story. This work may be defined in tasks or sub-tasks. All user stories likely have design and code work, and testing. Some may require UI design, database updates, API changes, and so on. Technical stories may require domain model changes, backend updates, code cleanup, and more.

> Note: There are entire books on to how to write good stories. If this area interests you, I highly recommend that you look at some of them. You can start with the items in the *Bibliography* on page 235.

User Stories

A user story is a single piece of functionality written from a user's perspective. Usually, the user story is written by the Product Owner.

The user story takes a feature or update that is planned for a release (possibly from an epic) and breaks it down into the smallest unit of work that will create a usable and deliverable piece of functionality. For example, as part of an epic for a log-in screen, the following might be the smallest usable unit of work:

1. **Username** field
2. **Password** field
3. **Show Password** option
4. **Forgot Password** link

Something to note here: Not all user stories that result from an epic are required. Stories 3 and 4 are considered "nice to have." Some stories might be dependent on others. You can't implement story 3 until you've implemented story 2.

User stories are generally written with a role (or persona), an action (a function or ability), and a benefit: As a [role], I want to [action] so that [benefit].

For each story, remember the Three C's:

- Card: it should be small enough to fit on the front of an index card.

- Conversation: The story is simply a starting point for discussions with the Customer or Product Owner and the Team members to elaborate the details.

- Confirmation: Every story should have unique acceptance criteria. This acceptance criteria is the minimum that the product must do to meet the needs of the owner.

Technical Stories

Technical stories do not result in user functionality. Rather, they are infrastructure or research stories. For a research story, a developer might determine if they can use pre-existing software for password validation or a module from another area of software in the company for the entire login screen.

Other non-functional stories include: knowledge transfer, learning, automation, technical debt, and my favorite, the infrastructure story. These tend to be written as "As a developer, I need to be able to ..."

These technical stories are often written by team members rather than the Product Owner.

For the Documentation impact and interaction, refer to *Stories* on page 162.

Tasks and Sub-tasks

Tasks and sub-tasks are optional. Their value depends on the team's method.

There is a theory that the better the teams get, the less likely they are to have tasks and sub-tasks. The idea is that the team members "just know" what to do and that creating and estimating tasks and sub-tasks is an unnecessary burden.

The opposing view is that tasks and sub-tasks allow more detailed and thorough tracking. Also, they provide a "team understanding" verification step. If someone creates a task that another member feels isn't needed, the team can discuss why it is or is not needed. Conversely, if the team leaves out a task that must be added, the team might need to discuss and re-size the story. For example, if a developer suggests a test task, it may be that they see an area of test that the QA team wasn't aware of.

If tasks and sub-tasks are used, they're created after stories are groomed and pointed. The tasks and sub-tasks must be created and estimated before the Sprint Backlog is finalized so that the time estimates can be used during capacity planning.

For the Documentation impact and interaction, refer to *Tasks and sub-tasks* on page 169.

Grooming

Grooming is an umbrella term for a series of processes that allow a team to determine the amount of work they will accept in the coming sprint. Those processes are:

- Story and Backlog Grooming
- Story Pointing
- Task Estimating

Story and Backlog Grooming

The Product Owner and the team are responsible for backlog grooming, which ensures that the product backlog items (PBIs) are ready for Sprint Planning. The team meets to discuss the stories, focusing on ensuring that the story is clear, the acceptance criteria is complete, any dependencies have been identified, and, if a story is too large, that it is broken into smaller stories. In addition, the Product Owner ranks the backlog so that the PBIs are in order of importance, or customer value.

> For the Documentation impact and interaction, refer to *Story and Backlog Grooming* on page 173.

Story Pointing

> Note: Some people refer to Story Pointing as "estimating" because they are providing an estimate of effort. While this is common practice, you should avoid using the terms interchangeably. Use "estimate" only for actual time estimates.

Story pointing is an area that causes a lot of confusion at first. Basically, each story is given a value based on the effort that will be required to complete it. This is not a time value or anything that corresponds to any timeframe. Pointing is based on relative size in comparison to other stories. You can think of them like t-shirt sizes. You're not estimating the chest measurement of the shirt. You're determining if it's x-small, small, medium, large, or x-large. It's important to remember that this is just an educated guess based on what you know; you are not held to this. Also, your ability to estimate will get better over time.

So, a team starts by finding a story that they will use as a baseline. That story should be a mid-level value, something not too large and not too small. (Fight your urge to reference Goldilocks and the Three Bears. The middle values are not "just right." Every value is right for its story.) Based on that "medium" shirt, the team points each story determining if they believe it is much larger (XL) or much smaller (XS). If a story is much larger than even an XL, then it is likely that the story should be broken into smaller stories. The team then allots a numeric value to each size. This numeric value makes it easier to provide metrics (and for entering values into a tracking system). I've seen teams point stories using fish (from guppy to whale), dogs (Chihuahua to Great Dane), and watercraft (canoe to aircraft carrier).

Once teams get a feel for story pointing using relative size, pointing is generally done using the Fibonacci sequence (1, 2, 3, 5, 8, 13, 21, 34, 55, 89, 144...) or a modified Fibonacci sequence (0, ½, 1, 2, 3, 5, 8, 13, 20, 40, and 100).

These story points are generally used for two purposes:

- Determining a team's capacity — The number of story points a team completes in an average sprint helps them determine how many stories you want to initially put in their Sprint Backlog. Task Estimating, discussed on page 67, fine tunes the backlog.

- Determining a team's velocity —A team should begin to complete more story points each sprint as they learn and adapt and hone their skills as a team.

For the Documentation impact and interaction, refer to *Story Pointing* on page 175.

Task Estimating

Unlike story pointing, estimation is based on numbers that represent real time values. They are used for capacity planning and sometimes for reporting; Story Points are used to plan a Sprint Backlog.

Estimates usually use the **Original Estimate** and **Remaining Estimate** fields in a JIRA story. These values are updated when you use the **Log Work** feature or when you close a story, task, sub-task, defect, or any kind of **Issue**, (These bolded terms are JIRA terms.)

Not all teams do estimation. Again, this will depend on how your team works. The point of estimating is to put an actual time value on specific tasks that need to be completed for the story to be complete. So, for estimation to work, you must have sub-tasks as part of your story. These might include: coding, CLI updates, API updates, developer test, QA test creation, QA test execution, etc. The person assigned to the sub-task, or someone knowledgeable about that area, provides a rough time estimation. When (or if) the team does capacity planning, to determine what they can do in a sprint, they will use these values.

"In the Sprint planning meeting, items on the Sprint Backlog are split into individual tasks. These tasks should take between 2 and 4 hours of work, with a maximum of 2 days" (Sutherland, *Power of Scrum*, p28).

If your team creates reports (such as burn-down charts), you may use *time* rather than *points* for those reports.

For the Documentation impact and interaction, refer to *Task Estimating* on page 179.

Sprints

Sprints are one of the key components of Scrum. As such, a lot has been written about them.

> For more information on sprints, you can start with the Agile or Scrum texts listed in the *Bibliography* on page 235.

There are three types of sprints:

- Standard Sprint
- Sprint Zero (optional)
- Hardening (Stabilization) Sprint (optional)

Standard Sprint

A sprint is the smallest unit of work time for a team, typically, 2 to 4 weeks. A release is made up of multiple sprints. There are some firm rules about sprints:

- The length of the sprint is inflexible. The sprint cannot be extended to finish work.

- All sprints should be of the same length.

- The team works from the Sprint Backlog pulling in the top PBI and working on it to completion, swarming if necessary.

- If the team runs out of work, they will pull from the top of the prioritized product backlog.

- The entire team meets daily for a stand-up meeting.

- The team must be left alone to do its work.

- New work cannot be added by anyone outside of the team during the sprint.

In addition to the rules above, the following *may* occur:

- Scrum Master facilitates issue resolution.
- The Product Owner may be asked to clarify requirements.
- A team member may demonstrate a feature or a part of a feature for other members of the team.

During each sprint, the team continues to refine the product backlog with story grooming and story pointing sessions in preparation for upcoming sprints. Any additional work identified during a sprint cannot be added to the sprint work. It must be added to the backlog and appropriately groomed and pointed by the team which then determines when to do the work. This is true for new stories and for any new defects that DO NOT block a current story from completion. Also, if a current story needs to be broken up into separate stories, it should be pulled out of the sprint and placed back into the backlog.

For the Documentation impact and interaction, refer to *Sprints* on page 181.

Sprint Zero

Sprint Zero is not an authentic Agile or Scrum element. It's something that many companies do when they're first starting off with Scrum and not all of the elements are in place yet. You can think of it as a running start. It is a time to do certain work before Sprint 1 that will thereafter be done during each sprint in preparation for the next sprint. In a Sprint Zero, you may find all or any of the following work being done:

- Identify any risks (not enough QA, knowledge gaps, hardware limitations, etc.)
- Review the Product Backlog
- Add stories if necessary
- Groom stories
- Point stories
- Determine the Sprint Backlog. In a Sprint Zero, you may not have a velocity. In this case, your workload will be based on the team's "gut feel" or on the experience of the team members.

For the Documentation impact and interaction, refer to *Sprint Zero* on page 184.

Hardening (Stabilization) Sprint

The need for, or use of, a Hardening or Stabilization Sprint is much-debated. When used, the point of this sprint is to allot a period of time for work to be done after code freeze. Basically, for small teams with small products, or for teams that have everything included in their stories and sprints, there is no need for this final sprint. However, in many situations, there is work that must be done after the teams have finished their work. This might include:

- Creating automated tests — Some teams do not have automated test creation as part of their Definition of Done, possibly due to available resources or other issues.
- Integration testing — For very large products, each team might create smaller bits of functionality. Testing how all those pieces work with all the other pieces from all the other teams is not feasible within the sprint.
- Long-term testing — Many larger systems have "soak" and other tests

that require running a system or systems at full load for a long period of time. If your sprint is two weeks, but you have a soak test that takes a week, you're likely not going to be able to complete your work and have it soak-tested within that two weeks.

If it is possible to do so, *without affecting the quality of the product*, all efforts should be made to avoid the need for this extra step. Frequently, that is not possible.

For the Documentation impact and interaction, refer to *Hardening (Stabilization) Sprint* on page 186.

Sprint Backlog

The Sprint Backlog is the collection of stories (and defects) that the team has committed to completing in a sprint. The team uses their known velocity (or a "gut feel" for the first few sprints), and their capacity, to define this backlog.

The Product Backlog can be updated at any time. The Sprint Backlog can only be updated before a Sprint Commitment. Organizations have different models, so updating the backlog can be done during the previous sprint, at the very beginning of the sprint, or between sprints (when your organization allows this).

Once the Sprint Backlog has been defined, usually in the Sprint Planning meeting, it cannot be changed without team agreement and only for a change that has been identified as critical by management.

For the Documentation impact and interaction, refer to *Sprint Backlog* on page 188.

Sprint Planning Meeting

By the Sprint Planning Meeting, all stories should have been groomed and pointed, and be "Ready" based on the criteria in the Definition of Ready. The team reviews any "late-breaking" issues. If a story is new and critical, and sufficiently defined, the team can groom and point it.

Starting at the top of the product backlog, the team adds stories and defects to the Sprint Backlog until the Sprint Backlog is filled to capacity. The team creates the task breakdowns for each backlog item. The team may need to revise the Sprint Backlog based on the task estimates and known capacity issues such as PTO, holidays, and team members being assigned to multiple teams.

"In the Sprint planning meeting, items on the Sprint Backlog are split into individual tasks. These tasks should take between 2 and 4 hours of work, with a maximum of 2 days" (Sutherland, *Power of Scrum*, p28).

After the team has agreed on the Sprint Backlog, it cannot be changed.

For the Documentation impact and interaction, refer to *Sprint Planning* on page 189.

Daily Stand-up Meeting

> The Daily Stand-up Meeting is such a key component of Scrum that a lot has been written about it. If you want to find out more, start with the items in the *Bibliography* on page 235.

The general consensus is that this is the most important meeting in Scrum. The Daily Stand-up Meeting (also known as the Daily Scrum Meeting, or just the Scrum Meeting) involves the entire team meeting every single day. The meeting should last, at most, 15 minutes, hence the "Stand-up" part of the name. (I've actually heard of a company that did Daily Plank Meetings where everyone was in plank position for the meeting. Good for your core, but I think I'll pass.)

In this meeting, each team member answers three questions:

1. *What did you do yesterday?*
2. *What do you plan to do today?*
3. *Do you have any blockers or impediments?*

That's it. That's why it shouldn't take more than 15 minutes. With a team of nine people, each takes a minute, and you're done in nine minutes. The Scrum Master's job here is to note any impediments or blockers and do what is necessary (after the meeting) to remove those obstacles.

Hard-liners say that there should be no conversation; each person gives their update and then the next person goes. (This is highly unlikely.) However, if a discussion goes beyond a minute or so, the Scrum Master should ask that the discussion be "taken offline" or "tabled" for later; some teams refer to a "parking lot". Many teams, especially distributed teams, schedule a 30-minute meeting. The first 15 minutes is for the stand-up meeting; the second 15 minutes is for "tabled" issues or for communications that might normally be done in person throughout the day but are impractical for a distributed team.

For the Documentation impact and interaction, refer to *Daily Stand-Up Meeting* on page 192.

Sprint Review or Sprint Demo

This meeting is attended by the entire team including all stakeholders; the Product Owner must attend. In this meeting, the team reviews everything that was completed. One team member demonstrates each story and the team determines if the story was completed in a way that met all the Acceptance Criteria.

Stories that are not accepted for release, or are not complete, are returned to the backlog or moved to the next sprint, based on the Product Owner's determination.

Frequently, groups external to the Scrum Team attend the meeting as well. These groups, including other Scrum Teams, use this meeting as a chance to provide feedback to the team and to gather information they need for their own purposes.

For the Documentation impact and interaction, refer to *Sprint Review or Sprint Demo* on page 195.

Feature Demo

The Feature Demo isn't a formal Scrum event. These demos tend to occur simply as a matter of course in the development of a complicated or nuanced feature. A member of the QA team might ask a Developer to demonstrate the feature, so the QA team can understand what they should be testing. Or a Developer might ask the QA team to look at a feature while it's being developed, to get the QA team's feedback or to point out extra areas that might need to be tested.

An in-team Feature Demo should not be confused with a Sprint Demo and should never be substituted for a Sprint Demo. Each story must always be demonstrated, to the extent possible, to all stakeholders so that they can evaluate it and ask questions.

For the Documentation impact and interaction, refer to *Feature Demo* on page 199.

Sprint Retrospective Meeting

Scrum (and Agile) is all about continuous improvement. The Sprint Retrospective is THE most fundamental way of making that improvement. This meeting is only for the Scrum team; no outside parties are allowed to attend. (The inclusion of the Product Owner is determined by the team.) At this meeting, the team reviews the sprint. They identify three basic areas:

1. What went well?
   (Because we're definitely going to **keep doing** that.)

2. What didn't go well?
   (Because, if possible, we're going to **stop doing** that.)

3. What would we like to try?
   (This might include something totally new, or just a new way of doing—or not doing—something.)

At the end of the meeting, the team should have a plan in place for things that they're going to immediately stop and things they are immediately going to start. The Scrum

Master will have a list of areas to help the team focus on. They may also have a list of things to bring to the attention of those outside of the team; again, the Scrum Master is responsible for removing impediments. If the Scrum Master cannot remove the obstacle, they will escalate it.

There are a variety of ways of doing this analysis, including simple discussions, exercises, and even games.

There are books and websites devoted to making retrospectives interesting and engaging. You can start with the items in the *Bibliography* on page 235.

For the Documentation impact and interaction, refer to *Sprint Retrospective* on page 202.

Bugs (Defects)

Bugs or defects are a given in development. If no one is finding bugs, something is wrong.

There are basically two types of defects:

1. A defect identified while a story is being worked on. These are part of the story and the story cannot be closed until the defect has been closed. If you're working in JIRA, these are frequently added to the story. In rare cases, the team may agree that the defect should be separated from the story and worked separately.

2. A defect found outside of a story, either after a story is closed or by another group working on another area. These defects are not part of a story in the current sprint.

   For the most part, these defects are handled in the same way as a story. They are groomed and analyzed ("triaged") and then added to the backlog. If a defect is critical, the Product Owner states that and moves the defect to the top of the backlog, so that as soon as the team is ready to take on more work, that defect is taken first.

In rare instances, the Product Owner may decide that the defect is so critical that it must be worked on immediately. The defect is pulled into the sprint and the team swarms on it. However, the Product Owner, and the organization, must acknowledge that regular sprint work will likely be impacted and therefore a story may not be completed in the current sprint. It is a trade-off that the organization must decide to make.

For the Documentation impact and interaction, refer to *Bugs (Defects)* on page 205.

Documentation in Scrum

Where does Documentation fit?

Now that you know what Scrum is, where does Documentation fit and how do you work in Scrum?

Some people have the extreme opinion that Documentation has no part in Agile. To support their argument, they refer to that third line of the Agile Manifesto:

"Working software over comprehensive documentation."

There has been a lot of discussion about this one line, but the fact is that this line refers to developer documentation artifacts (such as specifications, plans, etc.) and has nothing to do with (internal or external) customer documentation. Let me say this clearly: **This is not customer documentation; this is not you!** If you don't believe me, hit the internet. Every article you read regarding this statement concludes that this is about internal developer documentation, such as plans, specifications, and design documents.

A place for Customer Documentation

Let's be honest, the Scrum was not imagined and implemented with Customer Documentation in mind. It was imagined and designed for the development of software and hardware and, as such, it does not have a good place for Customer Documentation.

If you attend any Agile training, I would be willing to bet that you do not hear any mention of writers. We are not mentioned as members of a Scrum team. You'll see details for Development, Quality Assurance, Product Owners, and Scrum Masters. We aren't even mentioned as "stakeholders" either. They discuss Business Analysts, UI Designers, etc. But they never ever mention writers.

From Mike Cohn's *Succeeding with Agile*: "I will discuss the roles of analyst, project manager, architect, functional manager, programmer, database administrator, test, and user experience designer" (p137). There are a lot of roles listed there. Notice what's missing? Yep, writers.

The important thing to remember is that documentation products can and should be developed in Scrum. However, it is my assertion that a documentation product can also be a product unto itself and not a byproduct of another product.

Documentation may not be a necessary part of every product. There are thousands of products that are produced with little or no documentation. When was the last time you read the documentation that came with your smartphone? Did it even come with documentation? Did you use documentation to play a movie on your DVD player? Do you use documentation with your email application?

Of course, I am not saying that documentation is unnecessary. There are times when it is absolutely vital to a product. However, documentation is not necessarily produced or created as part of the product development process.

In *A Practical Approach to Large-Scale Agile Development,* Gary Gruver specifically puts Documentation into "Non-R&D Product Generation Activities/Teams" (p154), where he actually states that "These teams have started separating out key product information that remains static over the life of the product from common solutions that are always being enhanced and **need their own agile set of deliverables**." [emphasis added]

If you go to the "Technology" section of any bookstore (virtual or brick-and-mortar), you will find literally hundreds of books written **after** the product was already developed. In fact, this is the entire business model of the "For Dummies" series.

These books and other documentation products are created by incredibly talented writers who may have had no access to the product during its development.

You can most certainly create a product without documentation. And you can create documentation without a product.

It is my firm belief that documentation is an incredibly valuable product that is developed through its own process. The documentation development process can be complemented by, and benefit from, its inclusion in the product development process, but plenty of documentation is a separate and distinct product.

The truth is that customer documentation can benefit from Scrum. Being Scrum is perfect for us. We can be Agile, and we can be great at it. And it can make our lives so much simpler.

Your role in two different areas

The most important part of creating Documentation in a Scrum environment is identifying your role.

If you think of a Scrum team as a military unit in battle (and you can), then you should think of the writer for that team as an embedded journalist. The writer must work *with* that unit; we depend on each other. The writer is bound by some of the same rules as the troops, for everyone's benefit. However, for some aspects (much like a journalist writing and submitting a story), the writer is bound by their own set of rules. The truth is that the writer's work takes place in two separate and distinct areas (inside the team and outside the team) and each area has different processes, requirements, and products.

Within the Development Scrum Team

Within the Development Scrum Team, you're working on documentation products that directly result from the product being developed. You're an integral part of the Product Development process. You're an embedded member of that unit.

Your documentation product depends on the feature or stories the team is working on. If the team is updating an existing UI, then you will probably have a chunk of work for each story. In other cases, there may not be a one-to-one correspondence. If a team is building a section of the UI from scratch, it may not make sense to create a documentation product for each field on the screen as it is being developed. It may make more sense to have a single story that documents the entire screen. And, of course, there will be development stories for which you will have no work at all.

The method you use will depend on a variety of criteria and that is the main purpose of this book.

Within the Information Engineering Team

Within your own Information Engineering Team, you produce a wide variety of documentation products. You're a journalist.

You create all types of documentation products that do not relate to development stories. These might include architecture guides, workflows, Getting Started guides, and so on. We also work on documentation products that are not related to a particular product at all. These might include infrastructure work, style guides, and so on.

Within your Information Engineering Team, Scrum helps keep you on track, organized, and productive.

The Bare Minimum

Regardless of how you work with your Development Scrum Teams, there are three basic rules that will make your work easier.

- Have Documentation Impact indicator
- Don't start writing until QA starts testing
- Have your own Scrum Team

Documentation Impact indicator

All development stories need an indicator of whether a documentation product is required.

I've found it is best and easiest to create a JIRA field titled: **Documentation Impact** with options of **Yes** and **No** Impact.

(JIRA always includes **None** and you want to have a definite **Yes** and **No** option. If you have just **Yes** or **None**, you can't tell if **None** means no impact or if the impact has not been determined.)

Be very clear with your teams that, if they "flip that switch" to **No Impact**, there will be no documentation. The Information Engineering Team will not even look at the story. It's in their best interest to only set **No Impact** if they are absolutely positive that there is no impact. For example, they may have a story that is just a research spike, knowledge transfer, or backend change. Those wouldn't require documentation.

I highly recommend that your process requires that a story cannot be closed before the **Documentation Impact** has been determined. Teams don't always know what documentation products already exist or what impact a change may have on those products. This one step creates a safety net that prevents a world of problems later.

Don't start writing until QA starts testing

Whenever possible, regardless of your method of integrating Documentation, you should not start writing for a feature (user story) until the development is done. You can and should be involved in the discussions as the story progresses, but the actual documentation work should begin when the feature is stabilized. While this may seem like Waterfall, that's okay.

- QA can't test until development is done either.

- At that point, Development and QA should know how the feature works so they can accurately review the documentation product.

- Because Agile doesn't produce specifications and such, you don't have those documents to use a source. You can write from stories; however, starting that early may result in a lot of waste. Working software (or a demo of it) shows you exactly what to document and how it works.

- By waiting, you minimize churn. You aren't documenting something just to change it or throw it out completely when QA finds a problem.

Have your own Scrum Team

I said I wouldn't prescribe, and for the most part I won't, but I will say that **the most important** thing you can do is to create your own Information Engineering Scrum Team. You probably already have team meetings. Making yourself a Scrum team helps make your team more productive.

For the purposes of the remainder of this book, I'm going to differentiate the two teams you work on.

- **Information Engineering Scrum Team** — This is the Scrum team that the Information Engineering Team created. It is comprised of only writers and anyone included in the creation of documentation products.

- **Development Scrum Team** — This is the team doing product development. They create the product that you document. It will be comprised of Developers, QA, and all the folks who make up a "Scrum Team" in the Scrum world (*Scrum Teams* on page 50).

Regardless of how you work in your Development Scrum Teams, you need a place to do work not directly related to feature development. Also, some teams may not want the documentation work interfering with their velocity, burn down/up charts, story pointing, etc. You may end up with feature-related stories on your Information Engineering Scrum Team backlog. (We'll talk more about that later.)

Before you ask if you can have a Scrum Team of nothing but writers, remember:

- A team has stories. You do too. Whether they are for infrastructure work or for features, you have stories.

- A team is made up of everyone needed to produce work. Your team has just that. You may have experts on UI, API, tools, and so on.

It's important to remember that a Scrum Team can produce anything. A colleague created a Scrum Team when he remodeled his home. People have used Scrum to plan a wedding. In his book, Jeff Sutherland talks about how his son used Scrum to manage on-air reports from NPR correspondents in Cairo in 2011 (Sutherland, *Scrum: The Art*, p49–51). None of these produced software or hardware.

Roles in the Information Engineering Scrum Team

The roles in your Information Engineering Scrum Team are similar to those of any Scrum Team. You have team members, a Scrum Master, and a Product Owner. Those roles are slightly different within an Information Engineering Scrum Team as you'll learn below.

For a refresher on the Scrum-specific definition and description, refer to *Roles* on page 50.

- **Team Members** — This is the easiest area. Your team members are those involved in creating any and all customer information. This includes writers and editors, as well as other areas that may fall under that customer information umbrella, such as video creators, graphic designers, infrastructure and tools experts, and so on.

- **Scrum Master** — If your Information Engineering Team is new to Scrum, I highly recommend choosing your Scrum Master from outside of your team.

Your Scrum Master needs to be flexible enough to deal with the nuances of an Information Engineering Team but knowledgeable enough about Scrum to help guide the team.

If your company hires dedicated Scrum Masters and you can choose your Scrum Master, try to select someone flexible and willing to adjust.

If your company chooses Scrum Masters from within teams, I recommend choosing an experienced Scrum Master from within your QA team. They're accustomed to dealing with work that is dependent on another group. They're flexible in finding new ways to work. Yet they're meticulous enough to make sure that the team adheres to Scrum.

- **Product Owner** — Your Product Owner should be someone from the Information Engineering Team. Most likely, this would be an Information Engineering Manager or Team Lead. This person must represent your customer. That customer may be internal or external. Someone at a higher level in your Information Engineering Scrum Team is likely to have visibility into your customers as well as the infrastructure work that needs to be accomplished.

Methods

As I said, there are multiple methods for handling Documentation in Scrum. I'll go over each method, its pros and cons (and some possible responses to them, if you prefer a particular method), and a brief workflow showing some tips, tricks, and best practices.

These methods are not an "all or nothing" proposition. Try one and see if it works. Remember, "inspect and adapt" isn't just for software development. You can inspect and adapt your Documentation strategy as well. And, if you're on multiple teams, you can use different methods for different teams.

Basically, here are the three options:

1. Sprint Behind with a Related Story (SBRS) (refer to page 112): Documentation work is done a sprint behind the team and in a separate dependent story. (Don't freak out about being "waterfall" just yet.)

2. Same Sprint with a Related Story (SSRS) (refer to page 124): Documentation

work is done in the same sprint but with a separate dependent story.

3. Same Sprint and Story (SSS) (refer to page 135): Documentation work is done within the same sprint and within the same story.

Your first step in determining how you're going to work is to determine how your Development Scrum Team views Documentation. Remember, teams are empowered to do what works for them within the confines of the Scrum process; Agile is not prescriptive.

"Just as critical, but perhaps less celebrated, is the freedom to do your job in the way that you think best—to have autonomy. On all great teams, it's left to the members to decide how to carry out the goals set by those leading the organization" (Sutherland, *Scrum: The Art*, p 48).

So, ask your team flat out how they would like to work. And remember that, if you work on multiple teams, or if you change teams over time, always ask the team immediately upon joining. Different teams may do it differently.

Remember, the method can be decided by the team. It's what the team agrees to. So, explain the pros and cons of each method and help them decide what works best for that team.

"One of the key concepts in Scrum is that the team members decide *themselves* how they're going to do the work" (Sutherland, *Scrum: The Art*, p48).

While you will work with your team on deciding a method, you should also know which method works best for you. Before talking to the team, examine the following:

- Your product
- The size and makeup of your Information Engineering Team
- Your company
- "Customer" documentation needs
- The schedule
- Your support from management

Use these criteria and the descriptions of each method to determine which method works best for your unique situation.

Sprint Behind with a Related Story (SBRS)

This method works best when your documentation product is not integrated into the development product. If you have some piece of information that needs to be included in the product (such as online help or error messages), you may need to work within the same sprint or even the same story. Refer to those methods for more information.

However, it's important to remember that you are not limited to a single method. When you work, you can have stories that you work on in the same sprint, while others remain a sprint behind.

Pros

- **_Everything_** for the development story is complete by the time you start writing. This means that you can use the actual product, stories, and test cases to gather information. All of these are (hopefully) final and therefore present an accurate picture of the feature.

- The Sprint Review or Sprint Demo (refer to page 195) has provided information to enhance your documentation product. Any questions from the attendees and the answers from the team can help you clarify and highlight information in your documentation product.

- You can function as a second round of integrated "testing" for the new feature. While you're documenting the functionality, you're in an environment where it is completely integrated into mainline and you can identify any bugs or conflicts with existing features.

- You won't have to scrap everything you've written if they change the design mid-sprint or if QA finds a bug that requires a major change.

- The Product Owner has determined that this <u>is</u> what the "customer" wants. If it's not, the team creates a new story to change the functionality and puts that new story into their backlog. Meanwhile, because you waited for their work to be complete and accepted, you may not have to throw away your work.

- If the story is not completed and, therefore, the functionality is not included in the release, you don't have to go through your documentation product to find and remove only the information specific to that story. (Developers can "hide" their code; we may not have that ability.)

- Most organizations simply do not have sufficient Documentation resources to have a writer dedicated to each Development Scrum Team. If you have three writers, and 18 teams, there is no way for writers to provide the necessary coverage for each team. This method allows you to document the work of multiple teams.

Cons

- "This is not Scrum!"
  There are some teams that simply cannot get past the idea that this is Waterfall.

  o Your response: If you are doing this because you don't have enough writers, remind them that Scrum says each team member is dedicated to one and only one team.

  o Your response: Documentation is not required for a development product. Documentation is its own product. Some stories don't require documentation at all.

- The team may not remember the details of the feature when the time comes for them to review your document.

  o Your response: This is actually a rare complaint, but I have heard it. The response should be the same as it would be if someone found a bug in the software after a sprint is closed. The developer needs to refresh their memory.

- You may not have anything to do during Sprint 1 while the teams are developing functionality.

  o Your response: You have plenty of work to do. You start the infrastructure work for this new release: update documentation sets with new product version numbers and dates, set up new projects, branch your files, get new part numbers for all of your documents, set up your new timelines, move any information that was added to the release notes or in addenda at the last minute into the core documents, and so forth. As we know, there is a lot of work involved in resetting our work environment for a new release.

How We Work

For this method to work, your Development Scrum Team's output becomes your backlog. This is not unheard of. If your company does a Hardening or Stabilization Sprint or has an Integration period, they're perfectly set to do this. Basically, your backlog would be similar to an Integration Backlog.

When scaling a "system with components, like a software component and a firmware component ... we'll have a larger team downstream of both of these [software and firmware] teams that does system integration." (Clifford)

For an integration team, it is "just the 'done' items from the other teams that feed in and that comprise their Sprint Backlog." (Clifford) In much the same way, your backlog is the output from the Development Scrum Team, but you'll only work on the completed stories that require a documentation product.

Your Sprint Backlog

At the start of each sprint, generate a list of stories that the Development Scrum Team completed during their previous sprint.

It's important to identify what the team completed in their sprint. If they're not done, you should not commit to documenting the feature. You certainly can work on a story if you have time and you're comfortable with it; but you should not commit to getting it done.

Next, identify which of their completed stories require a documentation product. As I mentioned earlier, the Documentation Impact indicator (on page 98) helps identify the development stories that require a documentation product. Look at the Documentation Impact indicator.

- **Documentation Impact = Yes**
  For stories that have been determined to have a documentation impact, create documentation stories. This won't necessarily be a one-to-one correlation. One of their stories may result in

multiple documentation stories, for example, when a feature touches multiple areas of documentation. Sometimes several of their stories result in only one Documentation story, for example, when they have multiple stories to create a single feature that you document in a single story.

- **Documentation Impact = No**
For stories that have been determined NOT to have a documentation impact, I highly recommend scanning the list. Most likely, they're correct. The story might be about a backend change or just research. But have a look. You might notice something that they didn't know you document. In that case, change the determination to Yes, and handle it like the option above. You might also learn something about an area that is going to change in the future. If they're right, wipe that story from your mind. If there is something you want to keep an eye on, create your own story (research spike, or just down in your backlog).

- `Documentation Impact = Unknown`

  For stories where the documentation impact has not been determined, you need to review each and make a determination. Each story will fall into one of the two categories above. If it doesn't fit exactly, or the outcome still needs to be determined, my recommendation is to mark the `Documentation Impact = Yes` and then handle it the same way. This method keeps things from slipping through the cracks.

Add the resulting list of documentation stories to your sprint backlog.

Best practices

A best practice is to **link** the documentation story to the development story. If you're using JIRA, set the link so the documentation story **depends on** the development story. This allows a historical reference, a way of tracking the relationship between the documentation work and the development work.

If you have the ability to configure JIRA, you should create a field called **Documentation Story**, or something similar, so you can indicate in the development story which documentation story covers the work. Once you have that, you can run a query to identify all development stories that need to have a documentation story created, such as:

```
Documentation Impact="Yes"
AND Documentation Story is
Blank
```

Even better, if you can do it, is to set a condition so that the development story cannot be closed until the **Documentation Impact** field has been completed and, if necessary, that the related story has been specified in the **Documentation Story** field.

Your Sprint Commitment

Use your backlog and determine what you can commit to for the sprint. You can expect that, if you can't commit to completing all the stories that are linked to development stories completed in the prior sprint, you are going to get some flack. Simply show them your decision process, your capacity, and such.

Now you start your sprint work.

For the details about how to write, manage, and work with your Documentation Story, refer to *Stories* on page 162.

Same Sprint with a Related Story (SSRS)

This is the method that most teams start with because it is the middle ground between the two other methods and therefore allows for compromise from both sides.

It is also the method you should choose when the Development teams are already well into their Scrum implementation, but the Information Engineering Team is not; it allows the Scrum team to complete their work within the sprint, while it allows the Information Engineering Team to complete their work in their own way.

Pros

- You can create tasks or sub-tasks for the review process (create, review, edit/close). If the Scrum team isn't keen on cluttering up their stories with your extra sub-tasks, this can be an excellent compromise.

- The Development Scrum Team can close their story. This is usually the best selling point. Their work is done, and they can move on to the next story without waiting for you to complete your work. They can have their own Definition of Done that simply says, "The need for Documentation must be determined and, if there is a need, a documentation story must be created."

- Story pointing for Documentation is not the same as it is for Development. This method eliminates that issue. They point their stories their way; we point ours our way.

Cons

- This is not Scrum!!
  As I said with regard to the SBRS method, there are some teams that simply cannot get past the idea that this is Waterfall.

  o Your response: If you are doing this because you don't have enough writers, remind them that Scrum says each team member is dedicated to one and only one team.

  o Your response: Documentation is not required for a development product. Documentation is its own product. Some stories don't require documentation at all.

- If the Development Team doesn't close their story until the end of the sprint, we can't get our work done in the same sprint. Quite simply, you'll have to defer your story until the next sprint. A mature team should be planning their work so that this doesn't happen. An immature team will likely be deferring other things as they learn.

- If the development story, on which you based your story, gets to the end of the sprint and the story does not pass the Product Owner's acceptance (for whatever reason), you've wasted your time? Of course not. The documentation product or products you wrote will need to be tweaked just as the product is tweaked. They re-open their story, you re-open your story, and we all work together to get it right this time. Keep in mind that this is an excellent learning opportunity for everyone. "What did we miss and why?"

Under certain circumstances, more often than you might think, your documentation product or products can be used as a temporary fix. "We'll clarify the functionality in the documentation. Then we'll open a new story for the feature improvement."

How We Work

For this method to work your Development Scrum Team must have a firm sprint commitment and they must be clear with regard to which of their stories have a documentation impact.

Best practices

- A best practice is to **link** the documentation story to the development story. If you're using JIRA, set the link so the documentation story **depends on** the development story. This allows a historical reference, a way of tracking the relationship between the documentation work and the development work.

- If you have the ability to configure JIRA, you should create a field called **Documentation Story**, or something similar, so you can indicate in the development story which documentation story covers the work. Once you have that, you can run a query to identify all development stories that need to have a documentation story created, such as:

```
Documentation Impact="Yes"
AND Documentation Story is
Blank
```

- Even better, if you can do it, is to set a condition so that the development story cannot be closed until the **Documentation Impact** field has been completed and, if necessary, that the related story has been specified in the **Documentation Story** field.

Your Sprint Backlog

At the start of each sprint, get a list of the work that was not completed from your work in the prior sprint. Then add the stories that the team committed to for the sprint. However, of this latter list, you are going to look at the documentation impact.

- **`Documentation Impact = Yes`**
  For stories that have a documentation impact, create documentation stories. This won't necessarily be a one-to-one correlation. One of their stories might result in multiple documentation stories, for example, when a feature touches multiple areas of the documentation. Or, several of their stories might result in only one documentation story, for example, if they have multiple stories to create a single feature that you can document in a single story.

- **`Documentation Impact = No`**
  For stories that do NOT have a documentation impact, I highly recommend scanning the list. Most likely, they're correct. The story might

be about a backend change or just research. But have a look. You might notice something that they didn't know you document. In that case, change the determination to `Yes`, and handle it as in the previous bullet. If the impact is correct, ignore that story. If there is something you want to keep an eye on, "watch" their story or create your own story.

- **`Documentation Impact = Unknown`**
  For stories where the documentation impact has not been determined, you need to review each and make a determination. Each story will fall into one of the two categories above. If it doesn't fit exactly, or the outcome still needs to be determined, my recommendation is to mark the `Documentation Impact = Yes` and then handle it the same way. This method keeps things from slipping through the cracks.

After you have completed this review, add the resulting list of documentation stories to your sprint backlog.

Your Sprint Commitment

Use your backlog and capacity to determine what you can commit to for the sprint. You can expect that you are going to get some flack if you can't commit to completing all of your stories that are linked to stories that development completed in the prior sprint. Simply show them your decision process, your capacity, and such.

Now you start your sprint work.

You may need to adjust your backlog as you work. Be very careful. Some of your stories may not actually require documentation work; comment on them, close them, and move on. That is fine. However, if anyone asks you to add stories to your sprint commitment, be very hesitant. This is highly discouraged. A team should not add stories to a sprint unless they are done with everything else, or the need for the additional story or stories is critical and the impact of the addition has been analyzed and agreed on by everyone involved.

For the details about how to write, manage, and work with your Documentation Story, refer to *Stories* on page 162.

Same Sprint and Story (SSS)

This can be, by far, the most difficult method for the Information Engineering Team as it requires writers to create documentation products in lock-step with the team developing the feature or features.

However, it is the most preferred method by Scrum adherents who say that anything else is "Not Scrum."

Pros

- This is quintessential Scrum for those with orthodox Scrum ideals.

- The team must review the documentation products to close their story. So, you're more likely to get a review. It forces discipline within the other members of the Scrum team. In *The Power of Scrum*, Jeff Sutherland creates a fictional company (Logistrux) and characters (such as Mark Resting, CTO). Sutherland then uses these characters to explain the realizations that occur as the company starts implementing Scrum. Resting states:

"I was startled to realize that this 'Definition of Done' actually answered all the worries I had had about the lack of Documentation...If the DoD required adequate Documentation, that would have to be delivered within each sprint. This would be better; we used to document everything after the fact, when we were under the gun to deliver, and no one thought it was important... I could see the detail and discipline it would force us to undertake." (Sutherland, p94)

Cons

- Sub-tasks for reviewing the documentation product add significant overhead to a story.
  - o Assure the team that these sub-tasks are necessary for accurate and approved documentation products.
- Documentation is likely to be seen as the bottleneck.
  - o Here you have two options:
    - ▪ Work with them to identify and rectify the actual issues. (Who isn't doing their reviews? How can you better present the information for review? Are you not getting information you need from SMEs?) Don't get defensive. This isn't personal.
    - ▪ Recommend another method.
- Insufficient Documentation resources — If you have enough writers to cover your teams and their work, great! However, if, for instance, you have three writers and 15 teams, there is no way for each writer

to provide the necessary coverage for each Scrum Team. Each writer simply cannot attend the necessary meetings to identify what is happening during each sprint and document the resulting features within the sprint.

- Story points must include the documentation work and that is difficult.

  o Work with the Scrum Team to help them see the amount of effort writing and reviewing a story takes. Remind them of their review effort. Help them learn to incorporate these factors into their story pointing.

- Churn and waste — I'll confess that this is my absolute number one vexation with the SSS method. The writer creates a documentation product before the feature is complete and approved, writing as they learn and as the developers and QA learn. In the end, you might have a great documentation product that clearly records a finished feature. However, if the feature changes at any point during development and testing, which it almost always does, your documentation product changes. You may have to rewrite or even start from scratch. You may have wasted your time and effort. "No one should spend their lives on meaningless work. Not only is it not good business, it kills the soul." (Sutherland, *Scrum: The Art*, p11)

How We Work

The problem with lock step is basically churn, which results when the stories involve rework during the sprint. If your stories are too large, too complicated, or not clearly understood, they may be included in a sprint before they are truly ready. Including stories before they are ready results in refining, redefining, and rework by developers and QA and therefore by the writer.

Best practices

For lock-step to work, your entire process must be extremely tight and focused.

- The Information Engineering Team will not have its own stories for the work this team is doing. (You should still have your own Information Engineering Scrum Team with its own backlog.)

- Make sure the need for documentation work is spelled out in Acceptance Criteria for each story.

- Make sure that every story that requires documentation work has sub-tasks for creation, reviews, and editing.

- The story points must include the documentation work effort.

- Do not allow the team to commit to a Sprint Backlog that you cannot commit to documenting. I realize this may be easier said than done.

  If you don't have enough credibility and authority with the team for them to just take your word for it, then you might need to pull in others to speak for you. Consider the Scrum Master, Information Engineering Team Manager, and writers with more seniority.

  The other option is to let the team make their commitment. Then either you learn that they were right, or they learn that you were. You can discuss the situation in the Sprint Retrospective.

Your Sprint Backlog

In this case, your backlog is their backlog.

Your Sprint Commitment

In this case, your sprint commitment is their sprint commitment. Refer to the Best Practices above.

Documentation in Scrum Elements

At the beginning of this book, I provided a brief description of each of the elements of Scrum (stories, teams, meetings, etc.). That information provided no Documentation context. The following pages provide you with more details about how you implement those elements as a writer. The discussion of each element is broken into sections:

- A link back to the Scrum description. (Yes, this is first now so you can quickly go back to that information if you need a refresher.)

- A brief description, if necessary.

- "In the Development Scrum Team" provides information regarding if and how you interact with the team when they're working with the element.

  o Do you take part in their retrospective? [Spoiler: Yes.]

- o Do you take part in their story pointing?
  [Spoiler: It depends.]

- "In your Information Engineering Scrum Team" provides information on how the Information Engineering Scrum Team handles each particular element. It is critically important, regardless of which method you use, that you have your own Scrum Team (refer to page 102).

  - o Do you have a daily stand-up meeting?
    [Spoiler: Probably not.]

  - o Do you point your stories?
    [Spoiler: Yes; although "how" is a discussion.]

Product Vision and Roadmap

For the Scrum-specific definition and description, refer to *Product Vision and Roadmap* on page 45.

In the Development Scrum Team

You are going to need to know their Product Vision and Roadmap because that is the big picture of what you are going to be documenting. That big picture will inform your plan.

- How much work is coming up?
- How much of that work will require documentation work?
- Which documents will be affected?
- Do you have enough staff?
- Is your team correctly assigned to teams?

In your Information Engineering Scrum Team

This is basically your documentation plan. However, you should think of it more as a Wish List than an actual plan.

- What documentation products would you like to have for every audience?
- What enhancements and additions do you want to make to your existing set of documentation products?

This will give you a list of things to fill out your backlog during downtimes.

For more information on a documentation plan, refer to *Managing Your Documentation Projects* by Joann Hackos.

Epics

For the Scrum-specific definition and description, refer to *Epics* on page 46.

In the Development Scrum Team

You should review the Development Team's epics, so you know what they will be working on. At this level, you might be able to eliminate entire epics if they focus on areas that don't need documentation work. This can free you up to work on other areas or with another team or teams, for a sprint or even more.

In your Information Engineering Scrum Team

For the Information Engineering Scrum Team, you will break up your work into epics. Most likely, these epics focus on work not related to your work on the Development Scrum Team. Follow the structure of epics to create areas of work that you will focus on for the release. Be sure to prioritize the epics so you can work on the most important ones in your available time.

I've found that you can also create epics as placeholders, with no stories below them, for work that you think you may have to do. For example, if I'm currently documenting just the user interface for the product, I might create an epic for API documentation so that I can work on that later.

Product Backlog

> For the Scrum-specific definition and
> description, refer to *Product Backlog* on
> page 48.

In the Development Scrum Team

Much like the Product Vision and Roadmap,
you need to know what the team is doing to
know what you'll be documenting for them.
The Product Backlog is composed of all the
epics and stories the team or teams will use
to build or update the product.

Make sure you can access their product
backlog, so you can see their prioritized
backlog.

In your Information Engineering Scrum Team

Just like their Product Backlog, the
Documentation Product Backlog is the list of
your epics and stories.

Your Product Backlog should only have
documentation stories and epics. You

should prioritize your backlog based on what you want to do regardless of what other teams do. Think of it as a wish list that you create in a vacuum. If you had nothing else to work on, what would you create or update and in what order? Of course, your ability to actually do that work in that order is unlikely. However, as you move ahead with your work, this wish list will help you remember what you want to do or need to do next.

You will use this prioritized list to determine the stories that will go into your Sprint Backlog.

Scrum Teams

For the Scrum-specific definition and description, refer to *Scrum Teams* on page 50.

In the Development Scrum Team

Oh my, well, this is basically the point of this book. You're going to be on a Scrum team. How many teams and which ones will be determined by your company, products, and how the teams are focused.

If you are lucky enough to be on a single Development Scrum Team, make your best effort to attend all the meetings and ceremonies. The Development Scrum Team should be your primary focus and work for that team should be your priority.

Multiple Teams

Make your best effort never to be on more than three Scrum teams. With all the required work, ceremonies, and meetings, you'll be overworked and spread too thin.

This problem is exacerbated if all your teams do everything (such as Sprint Kickoff, Daily Stand-up Meeting, Retrospective, and so on) at the same time.

If you must be on multiple teams, make sure the teams are aware of all your obligations. Develop a plan with each team at the beginning of each sprint outlining the following:

- What is the team working on?

- What from their workload will require your attention? You may be able to skip working with a team for a sprint if their work doesn't require documentation work.

- Identify which meetings you will be attending and which you will not. Perhaps you'll attend a daily stand-up twice a week.

- Remind them of your capacity. How many other teams are you working with? Are there other issues that impact your capacity? Make sure they know how much actual work time you have.

- Create a plan for notifying you of anything you may miss by not attending every meeting.

If you meet with resistance, remind the team that, according to Scrum, each team member is supposed to be dedicated to a single team. I'm not the only one to say this. In an article about the heart of Agile, Sam McAfee states **"remember, if you're on more than one team, you're not on any team at all. Agile teams are dedicated teams"** (McAfee, 2018). By putting you on multiple teams, they are breaking with the Agile basics and they will need to make accommodations.

Distributed Teams

Scrum generally recommends co-location so teams can communicate quickly. If your teams are in different cities, states, or even countries, don't be surprised; this is quite typical. Co-location is one of the first of the Scrum ideals to be ignored.

When possible, use your skills to help the team overcome communications issues. If any of your team members have a language other than English as their native language, you are distinctly suited to clarifying communications between team members. You can volunteer to take notes and distribute team communications. I understand that just because we are writers does not mean we are excellent note takers, and that we generally try to avoid being a secretary to the team. However, in this case, you will be able to bring even greater value to your team. You can ask questions and "translate" (as necessary) information from one team member to the others. You can also volunteer to help foreign team members with their UI efforts (proofing or writing error messages, screen prompts, tool tips, and even field labels).

You have a certain set of skills; use them.

In your Information Engineering Scrum Team

For your Information Engineering Scrum Team, I have only one recommendation: Have your own Scrum Team. (For more information, refer to page 102.)

Definition of Ready (DoR)

For the Scrum-specific definition and description, refer to *Definition of Ready* on page 54.

In the Development Scrum Team

The team will (or should) establish their Definition of Ready (DoR) as one of their first team tasks, before the first sprint. Most companies have a generic DoR that teams then customize with their own additional criteria.

Work with the team to help them create a complete DoR. As part of that effort, you should ensure that the need for documentation is specified properly, if it is included. The DoR does not need to include documentation impact, but if it does you should make sure that the criteria meet your needs. For example, you might include a statement such as *"If there is an obvious documentation impact, that should be specified. If there is clearly no documentation impact, that information should be specified."* This indication is best specified in using the Documentation Impact indicator. For more information, on the Documentation Impact indicator, refer to page 98.

In your Information Engineering Scrum Team

Your Definition of Ready (DoR) should simply ensure that your stories have everything you need to start working.

Definition of Done (DoD)

For the Scrum-specific definition and description, refer to *Definition of Done* on page 55.

In the Development Scrum Team

Much like the Definition of Ready (DoR), the Definition of Done (DoD) is a key part of making Documentation work with Scrum. Stories must have a Definition of Done (DoD). This does not vary from story to story and every story must meet the DoD before it can be closed.

As the writer for the team, this requires your attention. The good news is that most companies allow each team to specify its own DoD. The company may have a baseline DoD, but each team will customize it to suit their own purposes. That means that you will be able to specify the criteria that you and the team have agreed upon, based on the Documentation Method you chose.

The reason that this decision matters is that you will be held accountable to this timeline. If the Definition of Done states that documentation work must be complete, then you will have to complete the documentation product for each and every story during the sprint or the team will not be able to close the story.

Try to have the team agree that the DoD simply states that *"The need for documentation has been determined."* Again, this indication is best specified in using the *Documentation Impact indicator.* (For more information on the Documentation Impact indicator, refer to page 98.)

If you are joining a team that already has an established DoD, I recommend that you review it. If it needs updating for your purposes, work with the team to come to an agreement.

In your Information Engineering Scrum Team

Set up your Definition of Done (DoD) so it specifies everything you need to close the story. Most likely, this will include items such as a review by the appropriate team members. It may also include a check-in to your content management system.

Stories

For the Scrum-specific definition and description, refer to *Stories* on page 56.

In the Development Scrum Team

The first thing to determine is which method you're using. For details, refer to Methods on page 108.

If you chose the *Sprint Behind with a Related Story (SBRS)* method (page 112) or the *Same Sprint with a Related Story (SSRS)* method (page 124), all of your work for the team will be in documentation stories based on development work. Refer to that method for details on how to do your work on the development-based documentation stories.

If you chose the *Same Sprint and Story (SSS)* method (page 135), your documentation effort for development stories will be done as tasks or sub-tasks within their stories. Refer to that method for details on how to do your work within their development stories.

Before you begin work, it is important to note that none of the non-functional stories (research spike, knowledge transfer, learning, automation, technical debt, and infrastructure) will require documentation work.

If you are also responsible for documenting non-UI functions, (such as API, domain, reporting, and so on), you should recommend that that documentation work be done in its own separate story. While the non-UI work might be required to make the feature work, these stories can and should be managed separately. Stories are often dependent upon each other, and that dependency is perfect for this type of work.

While you do not need to be too involved at the detail level of a story, if it is a functional story (one that results in a piece of functionality), you will need to understand the story enough to understand the functionality that you're going to have to document.

When the Development Scrum Team creates their story, you should use the story criteria to determine your documentation work. For example, the persona ("As a ____") in their story can equate to our audience analysis. The need ("I want to ____") helps you identify the feature and the area you will be documenting. And, finally, the reason ("so that I can ____") provides you with extra information to make your documentation product really useful; not just what the UI looks like, but what the user is going to do with it.

In your Information Engineering Scrum Team

The stories that your Information Engineering Scrum Team works on will depend on which method you chose.

If you chose the *Sprint Behind with a Related Story (SBRS)* method (page 112) or the *Same Sprint with a Related Story (SSRS)* method (page 124), you will have documentation stories based on development work in addition to your specialized documentation stories. Refer to that method for details on how to do your work on the development-based documentation stories.

If you chose the *Same Sprint and Story (SSS)* method (page 135), all of your stories will be specialized documentation stories; the documentation effort for development stories will be done in their stories. Refer to that method for details on how to do your work within their development stories.

For details on how to work on your specialized documentation stories, refer to *Specialized Documentation Stories* on page 167.

Specialized Documentation Stories

You should create specialized (overhead) stories to publish the documentation. For example, you may create a single epic for "Release Documentation" that covers everything, with a story for: each book, online help, each specialized extra document, and so on.

This provides several advantages.

- If your organization insists on logging and tracking time, the epic and its stories can provide those details.

- The epic tracks everything that must be done for each release. You can then close that epic for the next release. In JIRA, you can clone an epic. It doesn't clone all the stories. But if you have listed all the documents in the description, you'll know what stories you need to create. (You could clone all the individual stories and sub-tasks and just change the parent issue to the new epic.)

Be sure that these stories get to your Information Engineering Scrum Team

Backlog and then follow the same process you use for your feature documentation stories.

Tasks and sub-tasks

There are teams that do not work at the sub-task level, assuming that team members "just know" what they need to do. I am not convinced of the value of not having sub-tasks. Assuming a level knowledge is a dangerous thing.

Tasks and sub-tasks provide the team with a tracking mechanism, a method of determining how much of a story has been completed. Sub-tasks help the team members know what their colleagues are doing or need to do, which also helps in estimating and grooming.

> For the Scrum-specific definition and description, refer to *Tasks and Sub-tasks* on page 60.

In the Development Scrum Team

Your work with sub-tasks in your Development Scrum Team depends on the method you and your team choose.

If you are working with the *"Sprint Behind with a Related Story (SBRS)"* method or the *"Same Sprint with a Related Story (SSRS)"* method, then you will not have sub-tasks on their story. However, you should keep an eye on their sub-tasks to determine your work. For example, if there is a sub-task to update the UI, you know what you'll have to work on. Your sub-tasks will be on your stories. It is best if each story has sub-tasks for writing, reviews, and editing. You assign the writing, and editing, sub-tasks to yourself and you assign the review sub-tasks to the reviewers.

If you are working with the *"Same Sprint and Story (SSS)"* method, then you should have at least one sub-task to do your documentation work for the story. Of course, it would be better to have sub-tasks for writing, reviews, and editing; however, some teams want to keep their stories clean with a minimal number of tasks.

In your Information Engineering Scrum Team

Each of your documentation stories should have the necessary sub-tasks to complete the story. This may sound a little vague. The thing is that different stories require different types of work.

You may have sub-tasks such as writing, interviewing, researching, testing, editing, reviewing, publishing, and so on.

These are your stories in your backlog, so you can and should make them as robust as necessary, meaning that the story should have all the sub-tasks you need or want to make sure everything gets done on the story. I have stories that I re-use (clone) for every release to be sure that publishing, check-ins, posting, and so on are all completed for each document.

Grooming

As mentioned earlier (refer to page 62), grooming is an umbrella term for a series of processes that allow a team to determine the amount of work they will accept in the coming sprint. Those processes are:

- *Story and Backlog Grooming*
- *Story Pointing*
- *Task Estimating*

Story and Backlog Grooming

> For the Documentation impact and interaction, refer to *Story and Backlog Grooming* on page 63.

In the Development Scrum Team

When you're working with your Development Scrum Team, they will do their story grooming and backlog grooming for their stories. While the team discusses the stories, they are ensuring that they have everything they need to start working on each story, that it has met the Definition of Ready. Generally, this means that the story details are clear, the acceptance criteria is complete, dependencies have been identified, and, if a story is too large, that it is broken into smaller stories.

At some point, the Product Owner ranks the backlog so that the items are in order of importance, or customer value.

While the team is evaluating their stories, you should be evaluating the documentation implications. The method you're using will determine how you "tag" stories for documentation impact. (For details, refer to Methods on page 108.). Regardless of your method, make sure all the stories with a documentation impact or implication are identified and properly tagged.

In your Information Engineering Scrum Team

Within your own team, your grooming will be as much or as little as you'd like. You, of course, have stories and a backlog. However, that backlog and your capacity work on it, will depend a great deal on your workload with your Development Scrum Team.

I've found the best method is to do continuous grooming. Simply groom a couple of stories each week or each sprint so you always have a backlog of "ready" stories.

Story Pointing

> For the Scrum-specific definition and
> description, refer to *Story Pointing* on page
> 64.

In the Development Scrum Team

Story pointing on your Development Scrum
Team will depend on your organization's or
team's preference. My recommendation is
not to take part in their story pointing.
Unless you've been on a team and on a
project for a very long time, you won't be
able to estimate the Development and QA
effort for a given story. If the team wants
you to take part, do your best to understand
their system and point range. Explain that
your points might be outliers until you get
comfortable.

If you are using a method where your
documentation work is included in their
stories, be sure that the team considers the
documentation effort when they determine
the story points. (For details on the *"Same*

Sprint and Story (SSS)" method, refer to page 135.)

If you are using either of the other methods, you'll need to work with your team to determine if story points on your stories should be included in their sprint. I recommend against that. Your stories and story points may be vastly different from theirs and will likely skew their velocity. (For details on the *"Sprint Behind with a Related Story (SBRS)"* method, refer to page 112. For details on the *"Same Sprint with a Related Story (SSRS)"* method, refer to page 124.)

Regardless of whether you are taking part in their story pointing, you should attend their story pointing meetings. The discussions will help you get an understanding of the stories, their impact, their acceptance criteria, and so on. You can also attend to facilitate the process. You can do things such as counting down to the card flip (if they do that), or helping with discussions: "Taylor, why do you think the story is a 3? Parker, why do you think it's a 20?"

In your Information Engineering Scrum Team

Should you story point your documentation stories? It's really up to your team.

As I mentioned in the *Story Pointing* section earlier (starting on page 64), story points are generally used for two purposes:

- Determining a team's capacity — The number of story points you complete in an average sprint helps you identify how many stories you want to initially put in your Sprint Backlog.

- Determining a team's velocity —A team should begin to complete more story points each sprint as they learn and adapt and hone their skills as a team.

Before you decide to do story pointing, you'll need to determine if either of those functions is useful or necessary for your team.

If you decide to do story pointing on your team, you'll follow the same process as any other team.

Task Estimating

For the Scrum-specific definition and description, refer to *Task Estimating* on page 67.

In the Development Scrum Team

Task estimating is generally done at the sub-task level and not the task level. Each person estimates their sub-tasks on each story. If sub-tasks have not been created, each team member creates their sub-tasks and then estimates them. The estimate is in actual time not in story points.

The team then totals the estimates for all stories for each person. Each person's total is compared to their capacity for the sprint. The sprint backlog is adjusted until everyone is comfortable with their capacity.

If your team does documentation work within the story, then you will do your sub-task estimation in their story.

For more information on *Tasks and sub-tasks*, refer to page 169.

In your Information Engineering Scrum Team

Task estimating is not as important within your Information Engineering Scrum Team because your sprint backlog will fluctuate based on your workload with your Development Scrum Team.

In an ideal world, you'll determine your capacity to work on your documentation stories, determine which stories to commit to, and then complete them all within the sprint. As you know, documentation work rarely runs according to plan. So, estimate as you can. But know that your capacity is not set in stone.

Sprints

For the Scrum-specific definition and description, refer to *Sprints* on page 69.

In the Development Scrum Team

As I mentioned before, sprints are a key facet of Scrum. Some companies have sprints that are company-wide, meaning that all the teams start at the same time. If that is the case, it is going to be difficult if you're on more than one team. You can try asking each of your teams to stagger their ceremonies, meetings, and events. If they can't, or won't, then you must work with each team setting up a schedule and letting them know which meetings you can attend. You will also need to adjust your capacity to accommodate the workload of multiple teams. For example, if you have four teams plus your Information Engineering Scrum Team, then you should divide your capacity by five and tell each team that that is your availability or capacity for that team.

If your company allows each team to define and determine its own sprints, you will be much better equipped to handle multiple teams.

In your Information Engineering Scrum Team

If possible, have your own sprints with your own sprint schedule, and have them start **after** the Development Scrum Teams have started theirs. This lets you determine the team's sprint commitment. That information will inform your sprint commitment.

Sprint Zero

As mentioned earlier, most companies do not support the concept of a Sprint Zero. If it does occur, it is only once at the beginning of a release.

> For the Scrum-specific definition and description, refer to *Sprint Zero* on page 72.

In the Development Scrum Team

Your development Scrum Team will only use this time to get initial work completed. It's up to the team to determine what needs to be accomplished in this period.

If you need details on the work areas, refer to the other sections.

In your Information Engineering Scrum Team

You likely won't have a Sprint Zero for your Information Engineering Team. There is no real need. If the time is available, you can use the other information in this book to determine what you want to get a head start on.

Hardening (Stabilization) Sprint

As mentioned earlier, this concept is not always accepted and implemented. So, this topic might not be of use to you if your current company doesn't use it. However, I recommend at least knowing about it in case you change companies, or in case your company begins to implement it. Many companies do so when they begin to work with "Scrum at Scale."

For the Scrum-specific definition and description, refer to *Hardening (Stabilization) Sprint* on page 74.

In the Development Scrum Team

The Development Scrum Team will use this sprint for various kinds of testing: system, performance, smoke, full regression, and so forth. As they uncover information, you'll likely be adding it to the documentation product as release notes.

In your Information Engineering Scrum Team

You'll want to use this sprint for writing, editing, review, and publication. This can be tricky, especially if your team has very short sprints. However, if the sprints are long, you can break one of their sprints into smaller sprints of your own. For example, if they have 3-week sprints, you can break it into 3 one-week sprints of your own.

Sprint Backlog

> For the Scrum-specific definition and description, refer to *Sprint Backlog* on page 76.

The Sprint Backlog for your Development Scrum Team and for your Information Engineering Scrum Team depends on the method you and your team choose.

For details on the *"Sprint Behind with a Related Story (SBRS)"* method, refer to page 112.

For details on the *"Same Sprint with a Related Story (SSRS)"* method, refer to page 124.

For details on the *"Same Sprint and Story (SSS)"* method, refer to page 135.

Sprint Planning

For the Scrum-specific definition and description, refer to *Sprint Planning* on page 77.

In the Development Scrum Team

As I've said before, the team is going to plan their sprint with their backlog and their capacity. As they go along, make sure the team knows the impact their backlog will have on your documentation work and your capacity and workload.

I'm going to be honest here. Your capacity and workload may not be a consideration. They have their work to do and they likely won't be able to do much to alleviate your workload.

It's a very rare team that is so completely Agile or Scrum that they will reduce their sprint commitment to accommodate your workload. If you're lucky enough to have one of those teams, enjoy it (and be extremely nice to them).

If they don't have the ability to take your workload into account, and your workload becomes too great, you might try to guide them toward a method that allows you a little more time.

In your Information Engineering Scrum Team

I've found the best method for Sprint Planning within an Information Engineering Scrum Team is to always have a backlog with several sprints' worth of work. Make sure all the stories in that backlog are "ready" for anyone with the availability. Also, make sure that your Product Owner has prioritized that backlog.

You can, and should, put together the most basic Sprint Plan and Sprint Backlog. You should only assign the bare minimum of story points (or stories) to the sprint, allowing for the minimum capacity. This allows you to have a Sprint Plan that is likely achievable.

After the stories in this basic plan are completed, each person simply pulls the next story as they have the capacity.

However, don't be surprised if, at the end of the occasional sprint, you haven't completed even the basic Sprint Backlog. There are always other things that require our attention and things with a higher priority than our documentation stories.

I realize that not completing a story during a sprint is not Scrum. And setting a backlog that is a bare minimum and has no stretch goals isn't part of increasing your velocity. This isn't Scrum, but then again, as I've said before, neither are you. If you were, you wouldn't have the capacity problem in the first place.

Daily Stand-Up Meeting

> For the Scrum-specific definition and description, refer to *Daily Stand-up Meeting* on page 79.

In the Development Scrum Team

You should attend their meeting if time allows. This is your opportunity to help the team and help yourself. In the meeting, listen for updates on the features you are going to document or that you are currently documenting. Listen for opportunities to learn more about the features.

- Has the QA team requested a demonstration of a particular feature? If so, ask to be included in that demonstration.

- Is there an area or nuance of the feature that is causing difficulties for QA or the developer? Those might be areas you'll need to focus on.

- Is the developer talking about creating a mock-up? Ask to review it. You'll be able to get an early idea of how the product will look, and you'll be able to provide a user perspective on the UI.

If you cannot attend every stand-up meeting, be sure to create a schedule to regularly attend certain ones. For example, you might do one team on Mondays, Wednesdays, and Fridays; and the other team on Tuesdays and Thursdays. Also, put a process in place so the team knows that they should notify you of significant information and how to notify you.

In your Information Engineering Scrum Team

Clearly, if you are a lone writer, you don't need a stand-up meeting of any kind. But you probably already figured that out. If there are only two of you, you may not need a meeting either; your daily communication will suffice. You might set up a meeting if there are others who are interested in your output (though this likely would not be daily).

Regardless, the Daily Stand-up Meeting for your team most likely will not be daily. With all the other work you're doing and all the other meetings, you simply won't have time to do a daily update with your team. I recommend starting with a weekly meeting. You may be able to extend it to every other week. Discuss the stories you're working on and the status of each. Identify any blockers or problems you're having. Review significant dates and deadlines. Make sure everyone knows everything.

Sprint Review or Sprint Demo

> For the Scrum-specific definition and description, refer to *Sprint Review or Sprint Demo* on page 81.

In the Development Scrum Team

The Sprint Review (or Sprint Demo) should be attended, not only by the Scrum Team (Development, QA, and Product Owner), but also by Services, Professional Services, Customer Service, Customer Support, Implementation Teams, Training, and anyone else who is interested. These reviews have the benefit of providing the first look at the feature for the people who will have to demonstrate, implement, and support it for customers. They will have important input and questions. They'll ask the same questions that the customers may ask. They may identify areas that may require additional more-detailed documentation product. As they ask these questions, you can identify particular areas that require more focus. In addition, the

Developers, QA, and the Product Owner are in the meeting to provide immediate answers to those questions. The resulting dialogue can be invaluable for your documentation product.

In your Information Engineering Scrum Team

You might wonder what you can demonstrate. There are lots of things you do. Use this as an opportunity to market your team. Possibilities include:

- Documentation products you've completed. Probably not all of it, but maybe some of the larger pieces.

- Documentation products that are out for review. (Let people outside of Product Development know that you need or want their feedback.)

- Infrastructure changes (such as a new web-help layout or a new Documentation Portal).

- Work for teams outside of Product Development.

I also recommend using this as an opportunity to make your team more accessible to the rest of the company. Remind people that you're there to help. Offer your services to:

- Review the UI and error messages while they're still in development. Those for whom English is not a first language may value your feedback. (Just remember to promise confidentiality.)

- Review presentations. We've all seen those truly awful presentations that we cringe at. Don't let your company image be affected when you can help.

- Help the Training team or department.

- Review white papers and other Marketing collateral.

- Do usability testing.

Obviously, you only have so much time. But these small acts of kindness can pay off in a variety of ways to benefit the company, and sometimes you personally.

Also, I used to work at a company where we started including a segment called "The More You Know." (Yes, this was borrowed from NBC Universal's trademarked public service announcements.) Each Sprint Review we would provide tips for better writing. Topics included:

- That vs. Which
- Affect vs. Effect
- Plurals and Possessives (and Plural Possessives)

People loved these and we used to get tons of questions and suggestions for future topics. And everyone's writing got better.

Feature Demo

For the Scrum-specific definition and description, refer to *Feature Demo* on page 82.

In the Development Scrum Team

Make sure that your Development Scrum Team knows that you're interested in these demonstrations. You can provide the team with a great deal of insight before the feature gets too far. For example, you might see a user interface element that would cause confusion for the customer. It's better to point it out now than have to log a bug or, worse yet, have it get out to the customer, which results in extra calls to the support team.

Like the Sprint Review Demo, you will also hear details that will enhance your documentation products. Simple questions that QA asks might shed light on an area of the feature that requires more detailed explanation. Your documentation products can clarify and provide answers to those same questions, so the user doesn't have to ask them.

In your Information Engineering Scrum Team

You're unlikely to have a Feature Demo in your Information Engineering Scrum Team because you're not developing a software or hardware product. However, you might want to consider having a demonstration of a technique or process you're using. For example, JIRA offers a method to create multiple sub-tasks at one time. You might want to demonstrate that to the rest of your team, so they can learn from your research.

Sprint Retrospective

In my humble opinion, Sprint Retrospectives are one of the best results of Scrum. The basic idea is to allow for a safe place to discuss how the previous Sprint went. What went well? What didn't go well? What can, or should, we change?

This is a great opportunity for you to assess your methods. The key, regardless of the team, is to really listen to your teammates, so it's important to remember that everyone should leave their ego and their agenda at the door.

For the Scrum-specific definition and description, refer to *Sprint Retrospective* on page 83.

In the Development Scrum Team

If you're an integral part of the team, the Scrum Master should include you in this exercise. Look at this opportunity from two different perspectives:

1. You can be an unbiased viewer of their process and comment as necessary. When, as frequently happens, teams are broken into factions such as QA and Development, you may be able to provide a unique viewpoint from outside of both factions.

2. You can listen to your teammates and find ways to improve your process. You may find that other members of the team have different opinions about the work you're doing and how you're doing it. You might also identify areas where you need to work differently with other groups such as QA or Development. Use these meetings just as other teams do, to identify areas of improvement.

In your Information Engineering Scrum Team

This could be a short exercise depending on your situation. However, think about having a retrospective anyway. Talk with your team about what is working and what is not.

I recommend having this meeting only after every writer has had all their retrospectives with all their Development Scrum Teams, as you may uncover issues in those meetings that you want to raise in this one.

Bugs (Defects)

There are basically two types of defects that you will deal with as part of Documentation.

- **Documentation defects** — These are the typical issues you've always faced. Someone was looking at a documentation product and noticed a discrepancy. You'll need to handle these according to your standard process for updates. The only difference in Scrum is that someone may be filing a ticket in your bug-tracking system.

- **Product defects that affect documentation** — In some cases, a product defect may impact a documentation product. For example, if there's a problem with the way a field works, you may need to update your documentation product to reflect the new or corrected functionality. For these, you'll work with your team to identify the impact and make the necessary updates.

The most important thing to remember is that defects are just like any other backlog item. **They should not be added to the current sprint unless a decision is made to interrupt the sprint work for this.** And the decision-makers should be reminded that something else may slip. A team's sprint backlog and sprint work should never be interrupted unless there is a critical need.

I highly recommend that defect tickets should include a field that specifies whether there is a Documentation Impact. This will help you stay aware of these issues. (Again, JIRA queries are wonderful for this.)

Depending on which sprint you are in, the resolution of the defect, and your workflow (such as when you "freeze" your docs), these defects may end up in your release notes.

For the Scrum-specific definition and description, refer to *Bugs (Defects)* on page 85.

In the Development Scrum Team

If the team identifies a product defect that affects a documentation product, you will need to work with your team to identify the nature of the documentation impact and make the necessary changes to your documentation product. Be sure that the person who reported the defect reviews your documentation product as part of their verification process.

In your Information Engineering Scrum Team

Defects are handled just like any other item of work. First, verify that there is a work item (such as a JIRA ticket). Add it to your backlog. Just as you would any other item, groom and plan. If your company assigns story points to defects, then do so. When the time comes to plan for the next sprint, you can determine if the item can be assigned to that next sprint. Work on it when it comes up in your sprint backlog, not before.

Extras

Release Notes

Everything prior to this was about order and following the Scrum approach. With release notes, almost all of that goes out the window. Managing release notes is almost as difficult as herding cats. However, yet again, Scrum can help.

Hopefully, by now you understand the process you need to put into place for stories and defects. You'll need that process for release notes. The first thing I'm going to tell you is that the process will help but release notes are never simple or easy. Almost every company I've worked for has had some process in place but it's never foolproof and it never covers all the situations you'll encounter.

The following recommendations assume you are using JIRA. If you aren't, simply find an applicable mechanism in your software or in your process.

Release Note Required indicator

Like the Documentation Impact indicator, you should have a Release Note Required indicator.

Every bug (defect) must have the Release Note Required value set to Yes or No before it can be closed. Who makes that determination will depend on your situation? However, be sure that everyone knows that, if they set it to No, you will not look at the issue at all.

Run a query to determine which issues need a release note: **Release Note Required = Yes**

Unfortunately, for a Yes/No field, JIRA does not allow you to remove the default of **None**. So, I suggest using that to your advantage. Run a query to see if the indicator is still at its default value: **Release Note Required not in (Yes, No)**

If the indicator is still at its default of **None**, then it has not been evaluated and you need to forward that issue (or a list of those issues) to the Product Manager to review.

Release Note Type

You should have a way to determine the type of release note you're writing:

- Fixed in this Release — These are typically defects that were found by customers and fixed in the current release. I limit it to issues found by customers because you generally don't want to report bugs you found internally; no point in drawing attention to your flaws.

- Known Issues — These are typically smaller defects that might cause the customer some problem, but there is a workaround that allows them to continue with their work. If there isn't a workaround, unless it's just a minor nuisance, it should be fixed.

- New/Changed Features — These are typically stories that introduce new functionality. The amount of detail will depend on your product, but generally you should provide enough information for the customer to determine if they want to use the new feature and that they can get more detailed information elsewhere.

Release Note Text

Whatever you call this field, this is the text that will be put into the release notes. I highly recommend that you have someone else write this text. Some bugs are simple, and you can identify what was "broken" and how it was "fixed" but there is usually more to it. Your Product Manager might want to phrase it in a way that makes it clearer what the user was seeing and how it was fixed. Or, they may want to make it less honest to couch a flaw in prettier language. Regardless, there will probably be quite a few release note issues.

Starting from scratch. Help!

Most of the information before this assumed that there is a Scrum process in place at the company and that someone has determined that Documentation has a place in that process.

In some instances, that may not be the case. You might find yourself in a company where...

- They don't use the Agile or Scrum framework.

- The Information Engineering Team isn't included in Scrum at all or you're the first writer in the door.

Congratulations! You get to help pave the way. It's very rare that you get to set the foundation for best practices.

However, before you get too excited, be prepared for some push-back as you start to implement your ideas. It may not happen, but you'll want to be prepared just in case. If they're not really invested in Scrum, or convinced of the inclusion of Documentation in Scrum, you may have some work to do. You may face a variety of issues:

- They may not want to include you in Scrum teams.

- There may be too few writers.

- They may not want to review documentation products.

- The product is well into development and you're behind on the documentation products to support it.

- And so many more.

But, is that anything new for writers? Likely not.

If you meet with some resistance, figure out which method you want to use (refer to Methods starting on page 108). Next, find an Agile or Scrum advocate to be your supporter. Sell them on your plan and then get to work implementing your plan.

If you don't get any push-back, you're in luck. You can get everyone started the right way the first time without having to convince anyone of your plan. Determine the method or methods you want to use (refer to Methods starting on page 108).

Either way, start small and ease them into it slowly. I recommend starting with *The Bare Minimum* on page 97. Then create your own documentation-only stories for your infrastructure.

If they have development stories and are using them, you can start adding documentation tasks or separate stories depending on the method you choose.

If they don't have stories, create your documentation stories. Then I recommend initially starting with the Sprint Behind with a Related Story (SBRS) method outlined starting on page 112. That will allow you to get started documenting what they've already developed. (Of course, if they don't have stories and don't plan on creating any, then they're really doing it wrong. But that's a bigger issue than I can help you combat.)

Start being Scrum. Lead the way!

Other Areas to Consider

Helping with User Interface Design

While you may not be a user interface designer, you are a user. So, be sure to help them when they're doing UI design and messages. Help identify potential problems for users: confusing design, grammar issues, spelling, error messages, and so on. Anything the user sees, you can help fix or polish.

Being a Scrum Master

Once you really know Scrum, consider being a Scrum Master. Remember, a Scrum Master is, at the core, a facilitator. Many companies simply have the team pick their Scrum Master. So anyone can do it. You're organized and diplomatic, and you understand Scrum. So go for it. If your company hires designated Scrum Masters, they may still have too many teams. Volunteer to be a Scrum Master for one of the teams with a vacancy. If all of the teams have Scrum Masters, you can also volunteer to be a stand-in for the Scrum Master when they're on vacation, sick, or just double-booked.

Hackathons

If your company or your group has hackathons, join in. A hackathon is a multi-day event, sometimes as long as a standard sprint, in which individuals and teams work to create a product. The original idea was that the result should be a usable product. In recent years, however, teams have begun to create other things. For example, if your company develops cybersecurity software, a team might create an Asteroids-like game where players blast threats. Or, a team might create a utility that automates a tedious task.

Join a team if you can. I worked with a wonderful developer who helped create a utility that inspected the CLI (command line interface) code and generated files in our DITA XML format.

If you can't find a project that helps the Information Engineering Team, find a project where you can help. They'll appreciate the help and you might learn something about the product. If nothing else, it's a team-building exercise and it's usually a lot of fun.

Tips and Tricks

➤ When you work in JIRA, you can configure which fields are visible when you view a ticket. Do that! Configure it to show only the fields you need to see. You can change the configuration at any time. So, I tend to work in JIRA in chunks. I'll do all of my editing of certain fields at the same time. Then I reconfigure the visible fields and do a different type of editing. Remember, when you're done to set them back to default or you'll wonder why you're not seeing everything, or worse, you might not even know that you're not seeing everything.

➤ In JIRA, use filters or queries, a lot. They make your life so much easier.

➤ Set up "template" stories with everything you need for a real story. Then you simply clone the story and fill in the specific details. In some cases, this can even include sub-tasks. So, I set up a story for Final work for the doc set that includes sub-tasks for every piece of the doc set and includes reviews, publishing, posting, and so on. I have another "template" story that handles setting up for a new version of software. This one includes sub-tasks for creating new areas in my CMS; updating variables, version numbers, and dates; and setting up new stories for known work.

One thing to remember, currently, JIRA clones some information that you don't want. So, never assign the template story to a sprint; assign the cloned story. Never assign anyone to be a watcher on a template story.

➢ Find some way to have a text file that contains frequently used text. You might have a standard way of closing a story, such as "All reviews are done and edits are complete, as necessary." You might have a standard blurb detailing how and where a reviewer should do their review, or you might have standard email text you send when something is ready for the next step in your process. Whatever the text, or the purpose, if you find yourself typing the exact same thing (even with a small tweak) more than twice, make a copy of it in your frequently used text file.

➢ Find yourself a superb and functional text editor for editing your files. It won't be useful for anything that isn't text-based (for example, FrameMaker files) but you can (and will) use it for XML, HTML, text, and so on. You might even find yourself using it to figure out what a file is. I recently used mine to open a file with no file type. (Yes, I made sure it was safe.). When I opened it with my editor, the file type was declared at the top. The remaining file was gibberish. But by knowing the file type, I closed it, renamed it with the proper suffix, and opened it in the correct application.

My editor of choice is Visual Studio Code. Yes, it is intended for Developers, but you'll be amazed at how cool and helpful it is. You might need some time to learn it, but it'll be worth it.

Other weird Scrum stuff

Chickens, Pigs, what?!

If you spend enough time in an Agile company, you may hear references to chickens and pigs. According to the Scrum.org web site, "Ken Schwaber created the pigs and the chicken metaphor in the early days of Scrum and it has been used repeatedly to separate the people who are committed to the project from the people who are simply involved."

There are lots of references to the story but it goes something like this:

> A pig and a chicken decide they're going to go into business together but aren't sure what they want to do. The chicken says, "Let's open a breakfast restaurant; we'll serve bacon and eggs." The pig says, "No thanks. You'd be involved but I'd be committed."

The story is supposed to help define the roles between the Product Owner (chicken) and the team (pigs). So, are you a chicken or a pig? The good news is that it no longer matters because it was removed from *The Scrum Guide*. There were a variety of reasons. If you are interested in all the details, refer to the article written by Scrum Trainer Steve Porter (https://www.scrum.org/resources/chickens-and-pigs).

So, if your team wants to say "chicken" when you have nothing to contribute in a meeting, then feel free. If your team wants to do anything more with the metaphor, your best option is to point out that it's no longer relevant. You may have to point them to the new Scrum Guide for more details on the reasons it was removed.

What is a Pod?

Just when you think you have it all figured out, someone comes along and adds a new element. In this case, pods.

So, what is a pod? Well, that depends on who you ask.

At some companies, a pod is the equivalent of a Scrum Team, although it might be larger or smaller than a normal team.

At other companies, a pod is a collection of Scrum Teams that focus on a similar product area or feature.

For the purposes of your work, you should equate a pod with a Scrum Team and make adjustments according to your company's implementation of pods.

Scrum of Scrums

A Scrum of Scrums is an organizational structure put in place to manage multiple Scrum teams. This is only necessary in an organization with too many Scrum Teams to be managed individually, generally more than five Scrum teams. A Scrum of Scrums is a meeting for all the Scrum Masters of all the teams. Each gives an update on the status of their team. In addition, the teams talk about cross-team dependencies. This is where a team might identify a need for a specific skillset they don't have, or a team asks for a person to temporarily join the team because they're overloaded with work, or a team has extra capacity and offers to help other teams.

Bibliography

Agile

Cohn, Mike. *Succeeding with Agile: Software Development Using Scrum.* Upper Saddle River, NJ: Addison-Wesley, 2013.

Manifesto for Agile Software Development. The Agile Alliance, 2001. http://www.agilemanifesto.org

Mountain Goat Software https://www.mountaingoatsoftware.com

McAfee, Sam. *You Aren't Really Agile If You Aren't Doing These 9 Things.* LinkedIn. 11 August 2018. Retrieved from https://www.linkedin.com/pulse/you-arent-really-agile-doing-9-things-sam-mcafee

Ries, Marcus, and Diana Summers. *Agile Project Management: A Complete Beginner's Guide to Agile Project Management.* CreateSpace, 2016.

Stellman, Andrew, and Jennifer Greene. *Learning Agile: Understanding Scrum, XP, Lean, and Kanban.* Sebastopol, CA: O'Reilly Media, 2016.

Scrum

Rubin, Kenneth S. *Essential Scrum: A Practical Guide to the Most Popular Agile Process.* Upper Saddle River, NJ: Addison-Wesley, 2013.

Sims, Chris. *Scrum: A Breathtakingly Brief and Agile Introduction.* Foster City, CA: Dymaxicon, 2012.

Sims, Chris, and Hillary Louise. Johnson. *The Elements of Scrum.* Foster City, CA: Dymaxicon, 2011.

Sutherland, Jeff, and Ken Schwaber. *The Scrum Guide.* Scrum.Org and Scrum Inc., 7 July 2016. Retrieved from http://www.ScrumGuides.org/download.html

Sutherland, Jeffrey Victor., and J. J. Sutherland. *Scrum: The Art of Doing Twice the Work in Half the Time.* New York: Crown Business, 2014.

Sutherland, Jeffrey Victor., Rini Van Solingen, and Eelco Rustenburg. The Power of Scrum. North Charleston, SC: CreateSpace, 2011.

Stories

Adzic, Gojko, and David Evans. *Fifty Quick Ideas to Improve Your User Stories.* London: Neuri Consulting LLP, 2014.

Cohn, Mike. *User Stories Applied: For Agile Software Development.* Boston: Addison-Wesley, 2013.

Patton, Jeff, and Peter Economy. *User Story Mapping: Building Better Products Using Agile Software Design.* Sebastopol, CA: O'Reilly & Associates, 2014.

Vii, Paul. *Agile Product Management: User Stories.* CreateSpace, 2016.

Teams

Adkins, Lyssa. *Coaching Agile Teams: A Companion for ScrumMasters, Agile Coaches, and Project Managers in Transition.* Boston, MA: Addison-Wesley, 2010.

Broza, Gil. *The Human Side of Agile: How to Help Your Team Deliver.* Toronto: 3P Vantage, 2012.

Meyer, Pamela. *The Agility Shift: Creating Agile and Effective Leaders, Teams, and Organizations.* New York: Bibliomotion, 2015.

Miscellaneous

Clifford, John. "Scrum Boot Camp 2017." Dec. 2016. http://ondemand.construx.com/online-course/Scrum-boot-camp. Section: Scaling Scrum. (timestamp 3:34–6:02)

Cohn, Mike. *Agile Estimating and Planning.* Upper Saddle River, NJ: Prentice Hall, 2006.

Derby, Esther, and Diana Larsen. *Agile Retrospectives: Making Good Teams Great.* Dallas, TX: Pragmatic Bookshelf, 2006.

Hackos, Joann T. *Managing Your Documentation Projects.* John Wiley & Sons, 1994.

Index

D

E

F

S

T

U

V

velocity, 66, 72, 76, 103, 176, 177

NOTES

_____

_____

_____

_____

_____

_____

_____

_____

_____

_____

NOTES

_____

_____

_____

_____

_____

_____

_____

_____

_____

_____

NOTES

_____

_____

_____

_____

_____

_____

_____

_____

_____

_____

NOTES

NOTES

www.ingramcontent.com/pod-product-compliance
Lightning Source LLC
Chambersburg PA
CBHW051048050326
40690CB00006B/642